DANIEL

A STUDY GUIDE
COMMENTARY

Books in the "Study Guide" series . . .

DANIEL

A STUDY GUIDE
COMMENTARY

by

Leon J. Wood

ZONDERVAN
PUBLISHING HOUSE

OF THE ZONDERVAN CORPORATION
GRAND RAPIDS, MICHIGAN 49506

DANIEL: A STUDY GUIDE COMMENTARY
Copyright © 1975 by The Zondervan Corporation
Grand Rapids, Michigan

Fourth printing   1980
ISBN 0-310-34723-8

Library of Congress Catalog Card Number 74-11864

Printed in the United States of America

Contents

Preface

The book of Daniel presents two main benefits for its reader. In its historical section (chapters 1-6) it presents challenging truths and lessons for the Christian life. In its prophetic section (chapters 7-12) it gives significant, detailed predictions of the future, many of which are yet to be fulfilled. The purpose of this brief volume is to help the reader learn something of the value of both these benefits.

Here are some suggested helps for using the book for your study of Daniel:

1. Before beginning a time of study, ask the Holy Spirit to give you understanding.

2. Read the biblical story before reading the corresponding chapter in the book. The book is intended to be a study guide and help, not a substitute for the Bible.

3. Come to your study time with expectancy. The book of Daniel is interesting, relevant, and exciting. Be mentally alert to all that is there to learn.

4. Plan to give adequate time to your study. Think through the thoughts of the chapter and fix them in mind. When you believe you have mastered the content of a chapter, then tell the thoughts to yourself (or someone else) from memory. Afterwards, check both the story in the Bible and the comments in this book to see if you have left anything out.

5. Look for practical applications of the truths to your own life. Have an open heart to respond to these applications. This is the way to grow in spiritual maturity from your Bible study.

6. You will find significant help in your study if you read the articles in a Bible dictionary or encyclopedia as indicated at the close of most chapters in the book. There are also questions indicated there to aid in your study.

DANIEL: A STUDY GUIDE

Introduction

Background Information

Daniel stands as one of God's outstanding servants of the Old Testament. While still young, he was taken captive to foreign Babylon and there experienced major challenges to his God-fearing life, but he remained true. He provides one of the finest examples in all Scripture to follow. The stories selected from his life for inclusion in his book are filled with helpful lessons for the Christian.

A. Daniel's Place in Israel's History

Daniel lived at the close of the history of the divided kingdom of Israel. God brought punishment for sin at that time in the form of captivity to a strange land. Daniel was among those taken.

The division of Israel's united monarchy occurred in 931 B.C. Rehoboam became king of the resulting southern kingdom of Judah, and Jeroboam became king of the northern kingdom of Israel. The northern kingdom continued for a total of 209 years (931-722 B.C.) and then fell to the Assyrians. During this time, nineteen kings ruled, all of them described as wicked in the sight of God. The southern kingdom continued for 345 years (931-586 B.C.) and then fell to the Babylonians. It too had nineteen kings, but the average length of their reigns was considerably longer than of the northern kings. Of these nineteen, eight were considered good by God. But sin still abounded, resulting in the captivity of Daniel's day.

Captives were taken from Jerusalem to Babylon at three different times. The final and main time was in 586 B.C., when Jerusalem itself and the Temple of Solomon were destroyed (2 Kings 25). Daniel's time of captivity, however, came nineteen years earlier, in 605 B.C., in what is often called the first aspect of Judah's captivity. Among other captives taken at the same time as Daniel were his three close friends, Hananiah, Mishael, and Azariah (Dan. 1:6). A second aspect of the captivity occurred in 597 B.C., when some ten thousand leading people, mainly craftsmen and smiths, were taken (2 Kings 24:10-16). It should be realized, then, that Daniel had been in Babylon as a captive eight years by the time the ten thousand Judeans of the second aspect of the captivity arrived and nineteen years by the time of the main captivity and the destruction of Jerusalem.

B. Daniel the Man

Little is known of Daniel's life prior to the time of his captivity. He must have been of either royal or noble descent, however, to qualify for selection as one to be educated at the Babylonian court (Dan. 1:3); his parents must also have been devout people to account for Daniel's remarkable dedication to God.

1. *A righteous person*

Five episodes from Daniel's life as a captive are related in the first half of his book. They depict him as having many admirable qualities, but none more admirable than his resolve to live righteously before God. This characteristic is given significant verification by the prophet Ezekiel. Ezekiel lived as a contemporary of Daniel, having been taken captive in the second aspect of the general captivity in 597 B.C. By the time Ezekiel arrived in Babylon, then, Daniel had already been there for eight years and held his high position as head of Babylon's wise men (Dan. 2:48). Ezekiel certainly would have been quick to make inquiry regarding the young man who had risen to such a height of influence, likely thinking that he must have catered to pagan ways to have accomplished this. But Ezekiel discovered differently and was sufficiently impressed by Daniel to name him, along with Noah and Job, as a great man of righteousness (Ezek. 14:14, 20). This fact is still more remarkable when one recognizes that persons who live in a prior generation tend to stand out more prominently than contemporaries. Both Noah and Job, who were certainly outstanding examples of righteous conduct, lived centuries before the day when Ezekiel listed Daniel with them.

2. *Two main aspects of his work*

Because of the kind of person Daniel was and the degree of blessing that God was pleased to bestow upon him, it follows that God desired to accomplish something particular through him. Two areas of Daniel's work are significant in this connection. One is that

Daniel clearly was used to maintain the honor of the true God in pagan Babylon. Pagans of Daniel's day evaluated any foreign deity by the prosperity of the people who worshiped him and the size and success of their army. This means that when Judah was taken captive by Babylon, Judah's God did not measure up well in the sight of the Babylonians according to either standard. Their own deities would have appeared to be stronger. This, of course, was not pleasing to God, and He used Daniel to change the situation.[1] Particularly through the interpretation of two dreams of Nebuchadnezzar, the reading of miraculous writing on the palace wall of Belshazzar, and Daniel's deliverance from the lions' den in the reign of Darius, God used Daniel to bring adoration to Himself from the lips of these foreign rulers (see Dan. 2:46-49; 4:1-3, 34-37; 5:29; 6:25-27).

The other area of work concerns Daniel's enhancement of the welfare of his own people while they were in captivity. The lot of captives in a foreign land would naturally be expected to be hard and difficult, but this was not the case for most Jews in Babylonia. There is evidence, in fact, that they lived in good farming areas, had their own homes, enjoyed freedom of movement, continued their own institutions of elders, priests, and prophets, experienced adequate employment opportunities, and even carried on correspondence with people in their homeland.[2] The probable human factor accounting for this surprising condition was the influence of Daniel, working from his high position in the government. A principal reason for God's permitting him to be taken to Babylon, several years earlier than the main groups of captives, was probably to allow him to achieve such a position before they came. Besides this, Daniel may have had much to do with effecting the return of the captives to Judah in due time. He was still alive at this time and held the highest position of his career, serving under King Darius (Dan. 6:2, 3). That he held such a prominent place of influence is remarkable, especially since a complete change in government had taken place and he was himself more than eighty years old. God's hand in bringing this about is unmistakable and this suggests strongly that He had more work for Daniel to do. This work could well have been to influence King Cyrus to issue the decree permitting the Jewish return.

[1]This was much as God used Joseph and later Moses in Egypt centuries before. The Pharaohs of the day were forced to change their thinking regarding Israel's God (see Exod. 5:2) as a result of God's working through these two men.

[2]See L. J. Wood, *A Survey of Israel's History*, pp. 385-387 for discussion.

C. Historical Background of the Book

Because the scenes of Daniel took place in Babylonia, the historical background involved must be seen in terms of the history of this country. Most significant to the history is the world-changing battle of Carchemish, won by Nebuchadnezzar in the early summer of 605 B.C. Nebuchadnezzar was not actually king at the time, but, as matters developed, he became king before that summer was over. His father, Nabopolassar, had been struggling with the Egyptians for titular control of the Middle East for several years prior to this time, but in this particular year he was taken ill and had to remain home. The army was entrusted to Nebuchadnezzar and the young crown prince made good, soundly defeating the Egyptians, first at Carchemish and then at Hamath. When his father died before the summer ended, Nebuchadnezzar was made king; the date was the first of the month Elul, September 6 on our calendar.

The occasion when Nebuchadnezzar laid siege to Jerusalem (Dan. 1:1) and took Daniel and others captive was sometime between the Carchemish victory and this event of coronation. This is made clear by the date in Daniel 1:1, which states that the captivity occurred in the third year of Jehoiakim, Judah's king at the time. The final month of this third year would have been the month Tishri (October) of 605 B.C.,[3] when Nebuchadnezzar was back in Babylon once again. It could not have occurred after Nebuchadnezzar returned for his crowning, and so it had to be before.

For Nebuchadnezzar to have been able to make this siege of Jerusalem in the few weeks between his victory at Carchemish and his return to Babylon, he must have moved south quickly to Jerusalem after the Carchemish victory. He may have followed the retreating remnants of the Egyptian army for at least part of the way and then gone on to Jerusalem as the first of the western cities to be subjugated in his overall campaign to subjugate all leading cities of the area that had now fallen to his titular domination. Having come to the city, he demanded and received valuable plunder, including

---

[3]Jer. 46:2 says this siege occurred in Jehoiakim's fourth year. This seeming discrepancy can be explained. The Hebrews used two calendars, a religious one beginning with Nisan (April) in the spring and a civil one beginning with Tishri (October) in the fall. Thus an event occurring between Nisan and Tishri would be dated one year differently depending on which calendar system was used. Jeremiah was using the Nisan calendar; on that basis Jehoiakim's third year ended in the spring before Nebuchadnezzar's siege. Daniel was using the Tishri calendar; on that basis Jehoiakim's third year ended the following fall.

sacred objects from the Temple and also captives, among whom were choice young men like Daniel, Hananiah, Mishael, and Azariah.

It is quite clear that Nebuchadnezzar's interest in these young men did not involve punishment, primarily; his desire was to bring to Babylon the finest young men of his empire to train for important positions in his government. It is all but certain that he also brought young men from other subjugated cities to be educated and made available as possible selectees. Nebuchadnezzar did not have time that summer to make similar demands on many cities besides Jerusalem, but he clearly stated in his official chronicle that he came back within a few weeks to this western area after his coronation to continue the subjugating process.[4] In fact, he probably did not even have time to take the captives of Jerusalem with him on the first return, for he had to make a swift, special trip to get to Babylon for his inauguration day.[5] He did come back to continue his activity, however, returning to Babylon once more the following February (the month Sebat), 604 B.C. It was probably at that time that Daniel and his companions were brought to the great capital.

D. The Plan of the Book

The book of Daniel divides itself into two sections of six chapters each. The first section is historical, setting forth six outstanding stories from the life of Daniel and his three friends. The second section is prophetical, presenting four significant visions God gave to Daniel.

1. *The historical division*

The six stories of the historical section are very choice. It may be assumed that Daniel and his friends had any number of experiences that might have been told, which means that these must have been chosen by God as being especially significant. It should be realized that time moves quickly in this historical section, because quite a number of years elapse between several of the stories. Daniel changes in the book from a very young man to a very old one.

[4] For details of this history, see D. J. Wiseman, *The Chronicles of Chaldean Kings*, pp. 25, 69.

[5] The ancient Greek historian, Berossus, says that Nebuchadnezzar "committed the captives he had taken from the Jews, and Phoenicians, and Syrians, and of the nations belonging to Egypt, to some of his friends" so that he could hurry back to Babylon; quoted by Josephus, *Contra Apion*, I, 19; *Antiq.* X, 11, 1.

The first story tells of the captivity of Daniel and his friends and the difficult choice they had to make regarding food they would eat in the foreign capital. At this time their age was probably about fifteen years, for this was the approximate age at which young men of the day were chosen for such a purpose.[6] The second story tells of a dream of Nebuchadnezzar which Daniel interpreted. This dream came in Nebuchadnazzar's second year (Dan. 2:1), meaning that Daniel was then about seventeen. The third story reveals the faithfulness of Daniel's three friends in refusing to bow before Nebuchadnezzar's image and their miraculous deliverance from the blazing furnace. At least several years had elapsed since the dream occasion, for at this time these men already held government positions, received after their years of training. This event probably came relatively early in their lives, however, perhaps when they were about twenty.

The fourth story concerns a second dream of the king, one which Daniel also interpreted. This dream came toward the close of Nebuchadnezzar's reign, for it involved a period of insanity in his life lasting seven years. Since Nebuchadnezzar ruled forty-three years (605-562 B.C.), probably about thirty years had elapsed since the fiery furnace event, meaning that Daniel was close to fifty years old. The fifth story is about the miraculous writing on Belshazzar's palace wall and Daniel's reading of it. The exact date is known, for that night Belshazzar died and Babylon fell to the Medo-Persians (Dan. 5: 30, 31); this occurred in the fall of 539 B.C., making Daniel here about eighty-one. The sixth story depicts Daniel's being thrown into the den of lions as a result of a vicious plot on his life. Sufficient time must have elapsed since the previous story to allow for the new Persian ruler, Darius, to have organized his government (under 120 princes, supervised by three presidents, Dan. 6:1, 2). Probably about two more years had passed, making Daniel at least eighty-three. It should be realized, then, that the man thrown into the lions' den was no longer young but advanced in age.

2. The prophetical section

a. Four predictive visions. Daniel's first vision (chap. 7) occurred in Belshazzar's first year (553 B.C.; Dan. 7:1), when Daniel was about sixty-seven years old. The vision depicted four beasts, symbol-

---

[6]Plato (*Alcibiades* 1:121) says that the education of youths in Persia began at fourteen years, and Xenophon (*Cyropaedia*, 1, 2) speaks of the seventeenth year as the completion.

izing the succeeding history of four empires — Babylonian, Medo-Persian, Greek, and Roman. The second vision (chap. 8) was given in Belshazzar's third year (551 B.C.; Dan. 8:1) and represented a two-horned ram being crushed by a one-horned goat. The vision symbolized Greece, under Alexander the Great, defeating Medo-Persia. The third vision (chap. 9) was given thirteen years later, in Darius' first year (538 B.C.; Dan. 9:1) and concerned seventy weeks ("sevens" of years) of future Israelite history. Daniel was about eighty-two at the time. The fourth vision (chaps. 10-12) came in Cyrus' third year (536 B.C.; Dan. 10:1). (Cyrus was chief ruler, with Darius serving under him, both beginning their reigns the same year.) This vision portrayed both the Persian and Grecian periods.

b. Predictive significance. These four visions present in symbolism some of the most specific and significant predictions in all the Bible. Because of them, the book of Daniel has been called the book of Revelation of the Old Testament. They especially foretell history involving the empires during and following Daniel's own day. So accurately were the symbolisms fulfilled that liberal expositors have insisted the records were written after the history involved had transpired. All four visions concern also last-day events, still future today, so that the visions are of unusual importance for setting forth the main features of history yet to come.

E. Two Languages of the Book

The book of Daniel is unique in the Old Testament in having an extensive section written in Aramaic.[7] The principal language of the Old Testament of course is Hebrew, but in this book Hebrew is employed less than half the time, for the Aramaic extends from 2:4 to 7:28. The reason for the use of Aramaic is best seen in terms of the subject matter of the section where it is found. The material deals with matters pertaining to the Gentile world, with little notice of God's people, the Jews; apparently God saw Aramaic, the language of the Gentile world of the day, as being more suitable to record it than Hebrew, which was distinctly Jewish. This fact suggests a second form of division to the book. The first division noted was based on literary pattern, with a historical section being divided from a prophetical one. This second form is based on the identity of the people concerned. For want of better terms, the Aramaic section

[7]Two other Old Testament books do have shorter Aramaic sections: Ezra 4:8 – 6:18; 7:12-26; and Jer. 10:11.

may be called the Gentile section, and the Hebrew, the Jewish section.

F. The Author of the Book

Because modern critical scholarship denies the authorship of the book to its main character, Daniel, there is reason to examine the authorship. The main reason for the denial is that the book presents remarkably detailed history at least until the time of Antiochus Epiphanes (Syrian ruler, 175-164 B.C.), and liberal thinking holds that such information could only have been written after the events had occurred. Conservative students, who accept the fact of supernatural predictive prophecy, do not have this problem.

The book itself clearly presents Daniel as the author of at least the last half, because he is always the recipient of the revelations given, and he, as author, speaks regularly in the first person in these chapters (7-12). Also, in 12:4, Daniel is directed to preserve "the book," a reference to at least a substantial portion of the entire book, if not all of it.

That Daniel must have written the first half, too, follows from the unity of the book, as shown by several considerations. First, the two halves of the book are interdependent; this can be seen from a comparison of Daniel's interpretation of Nebuchadnezzar's dream of chapter 2 and the revelations given directly through him in the visions of chapters 7-12. Second, the terminology used in chapter 2, verse 28, and chapter 4, verses 2, 7, and 10, of the first half is similar to that of chapter 7, verses 1, 2, and 15, of the second. Third, there is a clear unity in the presentation of Daniel as a person throughout the book. Fourth, all chapters combine in the purpose of showing the supremacy of the God of heaven over all nations and their supposed deities.

For Further Study

1. Read articles in a Bible dictionary or encyclopedia (see bibliography) on: (a) Babylon, (b) Nebuchadnezzar, (c) Captivity.
2. At what time in Judah's history did Daniel live?
3. Why did Nebuchadnezzar take Daniel and his friends captive?
4. List the stories told in the first six chapters of Daniel. How old was Daniel at the time of the first story? How old at the last?
5. Give a title to each of the four visions seen by Daniel in chapters 7-12.

Chapter 1

Tested and Approved

The first chapter of Daniel tells about Daniel and his three friends being taken captive to Babylonia. It sets forth, more particularly, a difficult choice they had to make on arriving there, their commendable decision in respect to it, and God's consequent blessing on them.

A. The Historical Setting (Dan. 1:1-4, 6, 7)

The chapter begins with a description of the historical setting in which the captivity of Daniel and his friends took place.

1. Nebuchadnezzar comes against Jerusalem (Dan. 1:1, 2)

Nebuchadnezzar came against Jerusalem in the third year of Jehoiakim, king of Judah. As explained in the Introduction, Nebuchadnezzar was not yet the actual king but would become such before the summer was over. Jehoiakim was the seventeenth king of Judah, the eldest son of the pious Josiah. His younger brother Jehoahaz had been made king at Josiah's death (609 B.C.), but within three months he had been deposed by Pharaoh Necho of Egypt. Necho had the authority to order such a change because of his recent defeat of Judah's army at Megiddo, where Josiah was killed (2 Kings 23:29, 30). Jehoiakim did not prove to be a capable king. He was the one, for instance, who foolishly cut and burned Jeremiah's book, thinking that somehow this would offset its dire warnings (Jer. 36:23). He also squandered state funds to build a new palace unnecessarily, and for this Jeremiah, in disdain, foretold that he would be "buried with the burial of an ass" (Jer. 22:13-19).

The reason for the attack of Nebuchadnezzar against Jerusalem was given in the Introduction. He had just won titular control of a major part of the Middle East in a victory over Egypt at Carchemish, and he was letting Jerusalem know about this by a show of force. There probably was little, if any, actual fighting that took place, however (cf. 2 Kings 24:1; 2 Chron. 36:6, 7). It would seem that

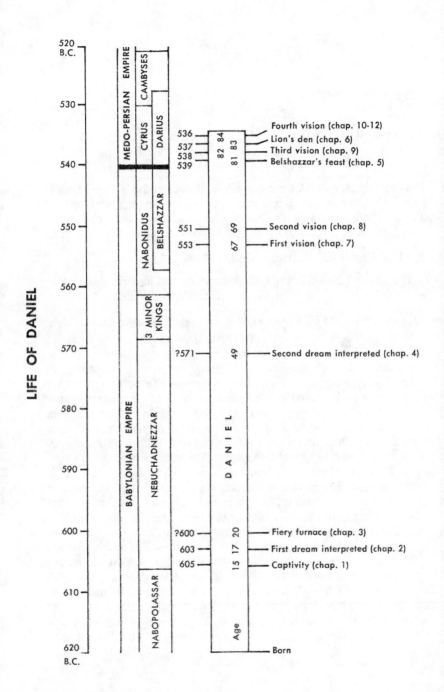

LIFE OF DANIEL

520 B.C.						

MEDO-PERSIAN EMPIRE

CAMBYSES

CYRUS

DARIUS

536 — 84 82 — Fourth vision (chap. 10-12)
— Lion's den (chap. 6)
537 — 83 81 — Third vision (chap. 9)
538 —
539 — — Belshazzar's feast (chap. 5)

BABYLONIAN EMPIRE

NABONIDUS

BELSHAZZAR

551 — 69 67 — Second vision (chap. 8)
553 — — First vision (chap. 7)

3 MINOR KINGS

?571 — 49 — Second dream interpreted (chap. 4)

NEBUCHADNEZZAR

D A N I E L

?600 — 20 — Fiery furnace (chap. 3)
603 — 20 17 — First dream interpreted (chap. 2)
605 — 15 — Captivity (chap. 1)

NABOPOLASSAR

Age

— Born

620 B.C.

Jehoiakim did put up some resistance at first, for he was bound by Nebuchadnezzar (2 Chron. 36:6, 7); but then he must have capitulated peacefully, for he was not taken to Babylon. In fact, he continued to reign in Jerusalem for another eight years.

2. *Two demands made (Dan. 1:2-4, 6, 7)*

Nebuchadnezzar made two primary demands on Jehoiakim, to which the King of Judah acceded.

a. The sacred objects of the Temple (Dan. 1:2). Nebuchadnezzar's first demand was that he be given the sacred objects of the famous Jerusalem Temple. Many of these had been made years before by Solomon and were extremely valuable. The word translated in the King James Version as "vessels" includes more than drinking containers; it refers to furniture and other equipment of the Temple as well. Several years before, Hezekiah had shown these valuable objects to messengers from Babylon, and at that time Isaiah had warned of a day when Babylon would come and seize them (Isa. 39). Approximately one century had elapsed since that warning (701-605 B.C.), and the prediction was starting to be fulfilled. It was completed in the later two phases of the captivity (597 and 586 B.C.) when more of the objects were taken.

b. Choice young men (Dan. 1:3, 4, 6, 7). The other demand was that choice young men be included among the captives taken. Ashpenaz, a chief among Nebuchadnezzar's officers, was directed to bring these to Nebuchadnezzar. The order may have been issued already in Jerusalem, so that Ashpenaz would have had the responsibility from the first in making sure that such young men were in the total group; or, it may have been given after all the captives had arrived in Babylon. In the latter case, someone else would have had to be sure that many choice young men were included when the group left Jerusalem.

The young men chosen had to measure up to high qualifications. For one thing, they had to be "young men," which probably means of middle-teen years, as indicated in the Introduction. The intention was to educate them and then select the best ones to fill important government positions. They had to be old enough to make the adjustment to a foreign land psychologically, yet young enough to learn easily and come to feel at home in a new cultural setting. Those chosen also had to qualify physically, having no bodily defect and possessing a pleasing appearance. Further, they had to be characterized by mental ability, having wisdom, knowledge, and power of quick comprehension (the phrase translated "understanding science" [KJV] means literally, "understanders of knowledge"). In other words, they had to have good minds. Finally, they had to have "ability to stand in the king's palace," meaning that they should have personalities that would allow them to live in a royal court without embarrassment. The last lines of verse 4 indicate a reason for the mental qualifications: they had to be able to learn the "learning" (literature or books) and "tongue" (language) of the Babylonians. The Babylonians are known to have had an extensive literature, and these young men had to master it; the Babylonian language, written with a wooden stylus on clay tablets, was difficult to grasp.

The purpose of this selection and this educational activity is indicated in the closing phrase of verse 5: "That at the end thereof they might stand before the king." "To stand before a king" means to serve the king (see Deut. 1:38; 1 Kings 10:8; 12:8). Nebuchadnezzar wanted these young men trained that he might use them in his court. It is reasonable to suppose that those who did the best in their educational pursuits would be the ones to receive the best and most responsible appointments.

Verse 6 states that among those chosen from Judah were the four main characters of the book: Daniel, Hananiah, Mishael, and Azariah. It is clear from verses 10 and 15 that others besides these were also included. And because of the defining phrase, "of Judah," it is likely that in this group were young men taken from other countries as well. Nebuchadnezzar would have wanted the best from which to make his eventual selection, no matter what part of his empire they represented.

Verse 7 tells of name changes for the four on arrival in Babylon. The reason, quite clearly, was to make them more Babylonian. Their former names were definitely Hebrew: the element "el" in Daniel and Mishael is one of the names of the true God, and the element "iah" in Hananiah and Azariah is an abbreviated form of Yahweh (Jehovah), another of His names. The new names given to them were equally Babylonian in character: Belteshazzar, Shadrach, Meshach, and Abed-nego. This change certainly must have been made by order of the Babylonians, for the young men themselves would not have chosen to have their former names taken from them. It should be realized, of course, that the whole situation was most unpleasant for the captives — being forcibly taken from home, friends, loved ones, and a familiar culture to live among complete strangers with a difficult adjustment to a new culture where a hard language would have to be learned. Especially for conservative young men like Daniel and his three friends, this must have been a distressing experience.

B. The Four Tested (Dan. 1:5)

On reaching the new country, Daniel and his friends were presented with an official order that made for a difficult decision on their part.

1. *Nature of the test*

The decision concerned a menu of food prescribed by the king. From the king's point of view, it was a splendid menu. It was to consist of nothing less than a "daily provision of the king's meat, and of the wine which he drank." The young men were to eat and drink the same diet as the king. This would have been received as welcome news by most of the young foreigners, and the Babylonians would have considered it an honor. It is quite clear, however, that Nebuchadnezzar was not thinking so much of honoring the men as accomplishing two other purposes. He wanted to provide good food for them so that his potential workers would be assured of good health; but, of still greater significance, he wanted to solicit their allegiance to the Babylonian religion. The king's food was regularly consecrated to the gods by offering a portion to them first. This was supposed to assure the favor of the gods for all who ate it. It also meant, of course, that those who ate it gave allegiance to the gods. Nebuchadnezzar's desire to solicit this allegiance is quite understandable, from his point of view. If these young recruits were to become good Babylonian workers, they should accept Babylonian ways, including the Babylonian religion.

Though news of the attractive menu would have been welcomed by most of the young men, it presented an immediate problem to Daniel and his friends. If they ate the food, it would appear that they were giving allegiance to the Babylonian gods. Such an action would nullify the effect of any testimony they might give regarding their personal devotion to their own true God. Besides this, there would have been the problem for them of the possibility of "unclean" food in this menu — food which God had forbidden them to eat. If they ate the king's menu, they would have nothing to say as to what kind of meat it contained. After the announcement was given, therefore, the four clearly must have recognized that they had a decision to make. As they walked back to their room, from what probably had been a general briefing session, they would have moved along with bowed heads and somber hearts. How would they respond to this order? How would they meet this definite test of their devotion to God?

The four may well have talked about the matter well into the following night. They had a decision to make, and it was not easy. They had to make a choice whether they would obey this directive or not. Decision-making, when the decision is important, is never easy, but it is probably the most important thing a Christian ever does. In so many situations, to decide one way is to do the will of God, while to decide the other is to disobey Him. The way a person chooses each time is crucial to his Christian walk. The manner of his decision testifies what kind of Christian he is, and it also predicts what kind of Christian he will be tomorrow; for people shape the degree of spiritual maturity they will show in the future by how they decide today.

2. Difficulty of the test

Decisions are difficult in proportion to the attractions that exist for making the wrong decision. It is important to take time here to notice some of the attractions these four teen-agers faced as they made their decision.

First, there was the fact that the king had ordered this menu to be eaten. It had not merely been made available; it was the king's command that they eat it. This is evidenced by the word used in this connection, "appointed" (Dan. 1:5), and also by the fear displayed by the king's officer when Daniel asked to have a substitute diet provided (Dan. 1:10). Normally, God's people are to obey the laws under which they live. There is only one exception: when the earthly law directly contradicts God's law (see Acts 5:29). This was the case here, which the young men surely realized. But it would have been easy for them to have rationalized that they really had no choice because a binding regulation had been given.

Second, they must have realized that disobedience to such a regulation could bring severe punishment. Punishments of the time were not light, as witnessed by the fiery furnace of Daniel 3 and the den of lions in Daniel 6. Punishments of such a kind would have been nothing less than terrifying to contemplate.

Third, the menu presented would have appealed strongly to the natural appetites of four young men. Being the king's own menu, it could be expected to include only the finest food. It would be composed of tasty dishes, always prepared in the most attractive manner. In contrast, if they chose not to eat it, they would have vegetables and water (v. 12). What a factor this would have been in a choice by four normal teen-age boys!

Fourth, disobedience to the order, even if the four were unable to avoid the punishment, could work to their great disadvantage in respect to future positions. The four would have wanted to do well in their new situation, but to begin by refusing the first order given seemed like getting off to the worst start possible. Rather than having a chance at the better positions at the end, they would be fortunate to receive any at all.

Fifth, there would have been a temptation to reason that because God had not been good to them (as it seemed) in permitting them to be taken captive from their homes, they did not have to be so careful in their obedience to Him. They had not wanted to come here where this temptation was now placed before them; why, then, did they have to make the decision to turn the attraction down? Why should they not eat and enjoy this fine food along with the other young men?

Sixth, it is quite possible, if not probable, that the parents of all four of these young men were still back in Jerusalem. If so, the temptation to do wrong in this decision would have been increased by the fact that "Mom and Dad" would never know. Christians often show their degree of dedication most clearly when they are away from home, when those who know them best will not know what they are doing.

C. The Admirable Decision (Dan. 1:8-16)

1. *The decision made (Dan. 1:8)*

It would have been interesting to listen in on the discussion of Daniel and his friends as they talked about these matters that night. The various attractions would have been mentioned and considered one by one. No doubt, some difference of opinion was expressed from time to time, but finally each attraction was set aside and turned down. This is indicated particularly by verse 8: "But Daniel purposed in his heart that he would not defile himself." The context of the verse clearly shows that the other three purposed the same thing, but Daniel was the leader and he alone is mentioned. The use of the word "defile" demonstrates the truth of what has been said: the four would have been defiling themselves if they had accepted the menu and eaten it.

2. *The decision carried out (Dan. 1:8-10)*

It is one thing to make a decision, and it is another to carry it out. Too many good decisions, made earnestly, are never put into effect. Daniel further sets a fine example in moving ahead without delay to carry out his decision.

He went to the "prince of the eunuchs" (very likely Ashpenaz), the assigned supervisor, and requested "that he might not defile himself." To do this was not easy, either. No doubt Daniel had to make an appointment with the important official. He might have reasoned that such a person would never listen to him. He might think Daniel was ungrateful for the benefit being provided in the menu. The man might even ridicule him or perhaps have him summarily dispatched. But Daniel did not let any such thoughts deter him. He did what was necessary to see the man and present the request.

A further significant thought is suggested by the words Daniel used: "that he might not defile himself." To have spoken of the menu as bringing defilement would have called for a testimony to Daniel's faith in his God. Daniel must have realized this from the start, which means that he intended to give the testimony. Daniel was not ashamed of his faith, even in pagan Babylon, talking to one of the court's high officials. It should not be overlooked that for Daniel to speak of this food as defiling to himself could have been considered insulting to the Babylonian generosity. Daniel no doubt recognized this and tried to offset such an implication by proper explanations; but the fact of the implication was an additional factor that Daniel had to decide to risk in going ahead with the request.

At this point (v. 9), the text presents an important thought, almost parenthetically: "Now God had brought Daniel into favour and tender love with the prince of the eunuchs." The significance is evident. One reason that Daniel had the courage to see this man, and a main reason why the man was willing to receive Daniel kindly, was because of the reputation Daniel had gained in his sight: Daniel had been brought into his favor. When or how this happened is not indicated; perhaps it was on the long trek from Jerusalem to Babylon. At least sometime Daniel had been able to be of help to Ashpenaz and had demonstrated the kind of young man he was. Reputation is so very important. Daniel's fine reputation became of great significance at this time.

But though this officer did favor Daniel, he still did not feel he could accede to the request. He did answer Daniel kindly, in keeping with the favor he felt, but he did not tell Daniel he could have a substitute menu. The thrust of his reply was that to do so would be to endanger his own life before the king. If the king should see the four young men looking worse than the others, he would want to know why. This would reveal the fact of the substitution and Ashpenaz's disregard of the order.

3. *A suggested alternative (Dan. 1:11-13)*

At this point, Daniel might easily have ceased his efforts. If he had been looking for an excuse not to carry through with his decision, he had one now. He had actually gone to the proper official and been turned down. He had tried to effect the request, but it had proved impossible. Therefore, the four would have to obey the king's order. This is the way so many of God's children would have reasoned, but not Daniel. He worked out an alternative method by which to have the request granted and he put it into effect.

The alternative was to suggest a trial period of ten days to see if the four would suffer any loss by a substitute menu. He presented this suggestion to one called "Melzar," or perhaps better, "the melzar." A definite article is used with the word, suggesting that it refers to some type of office rather than a man's name. The man served under Ashpenaz (v. 11), and Daniel found it advisable for some reason to work through him. Daniel asked him to test the four friends for ten days, giving them pulse (food that grows from seeds, primarily vegetables) and water, and then to make his decision whether they were physically worse than the others or not.

Daniel showed good sense in this manner of suggestion, for it was a type of test that the melzar could hardly refuse. After all, what harm could come in ten days? No doubt, Daniel had set the time purposely short so the man would not be able to refuse. Sometimes Christians complain that officials of the world will not cooperate with their programs, when really the fault lies with themselves because they have not presented a proposal the person could understand or find possible to accept from his point of view. Daniel did, however. Daniel's suggestion also displayed great faith. Not only would the four young men have to look no worse than the others at the end of the test period, but they would actually have to look better if this Babylonian officer was to be convinced. He could too easily imagine them to be poorer otherwise, even if they were not. A period of ten days was a short time for God to effect much of an improvement, but Daniel evidently believed God would bring it about.

4. *The suggestion accepted (Dan. 1:14-16)*

When Christians put God's interest first, God blesses them. Christ said, "But seek ye first the kingdom of God, and his righteousness; and all these things shall be added unto you" (Matt. 6:33). God now blessed Daniel and his friends.

Because Daniel's suggestion was as wise as it was, the melzar accepted it. It is also quite possible that he, like Ashpenaz, felt favor for Daniel and therefore wanted to respond affirmatively if he could. He could see no possible danger to himself in letting the four eat what they wanted for ten days. However, to work out this special situation for the young men would take extra effort on his part. Appropriate instructions would have to be given to the kitchen, and he likely would have to arrange for them to eat in a separate dining area from the others. Still, he acceded. Surely God intervened on behalf of the four to incline this man's heart in such a manner.

For ten days, then, the four ate the special diet. It should be realized that this was not easy for them, either. While the other trainees were in the main dining room eating the finest Babylonian dishes, they were in their separate room, eating vegetables. Not only was there the difference in type of food, but the others, including those who waited on them, would have thought them strange and probably stupid. How could anyone be in his right mind and call for a substitute menu of this kind? But the four stayed with their humble food all ten days.

When the ten days were over, the melzar made his judgment concerning their condition. He probably had watched them closely all during the time, too, but it was on the agreed tenth day that the decision was made. He found them "fairer and fatter in flesh" than any of the others. It took faith on Daniel's part to believe that God would do this, and God met him in that faith. The Christian may always be sure that God will never fail him. There is often failure on the Christian's part, but never on God's. Remember, too, that Daniel was yet in his middle teens. Sometimes it is thought that young people cannot really exercise faith. They can, however, just as Daniel did.

The result was that the melzar continued to take away the king's menu and substitute the vegetable diet. It should be noticed that no indication is given at this point that he decided to do this for the full three years. Very likely the decision was merely to continue the substitution on a day-to-day basis. It may be assumed that if the melzar had noticed any change for the worse at any time, he would have desisted immediately. Daniel and his friends were pleased with this result, of course, but at the same time, it meant the continuation of their humiliating distinction from the other young men. And this distinction was not for merely another ten days, but for three full years. It must not have been easy to contemplate experiencing the jeers and taunts that would come their way for such a length of time, but they still showed themselves willing to go through with their decision for God.

D. God's Favor on the Four Youths (Dan. 1:17-21)

The last five verses of the chapter indicate the result of the fine choice the four made. Rather than suffering punishment at the hands of an angry king or experiencing any loss in their competition with the other young men, they actually were advanced in position above the others.

1. *The immediate result (Dan. 1:17)*

The immediate result — that which was experienced as the days of the three years passed — is noted first. The four were given "knowledge and skill in all learning and wisdom." The word translated "learning" is again the word for "books," and doubtless the reference is to a mastery of Babylonian literature. Though the four had to be different from the others in what they ate, they did not in their intellectual activity. In fact, they may well have given themselves all the more diligently in this respect because of the seeming disadvantage of their special eating arrangement. Though the text says that God gave them their knowledge, skill, and wisdom, it should be remembered that God regularly uses means to accomplish His purpose. The means in this instance were long hours of study. God was the one who gave the four their fine progress, of course, but He did so only as they did all they could by His help to bring it about. God has given His children natural faculties, and He expects these to be used if He is to provide the desired blessing. This is always true.

In addition to what Daniel's three friends achieved, Daniel himself was given "understanding in all visions and dreams." This ability was imparted by God on a special basis, apart from any possible human study or effort. There was no technique in this respect that

Daniel could learn by himself. It is important to note this fact, for the Babylonians believed that one could learn to interpret dreams. In fact, much of the literature in which the young men had to become proficient concerned such pagan techniques. Methods of divination had been devised and serious attention was given to these methods by specialists. These methods had to be rejected by the four. One reason for mentioning Daniel's special gift may be to show that they did reject them and that that was why God gave Daniel special insight for interpreting visions and dreams. Another reason, of course, is to prepare the reader for Daniel's activity in giving such interpretations more than once in the following chapters of the book.

2. *The later result (Dan. 1:18-21)*

Verse 18 concerns the examination given all the young men on the completion of the three-year course of study. Each, perhaps individually or in groups, was brought before Nebuchadnezzar for the king's personal evaluation. The occasion would have been crucial for each one, for he would find out what place in the government he would receive. It was especially important to Daniel and his friends, for this was when any possible physical defect due to their substitute diet would show, as well as the results of their hard work in study. It was significant even for Ashpenaz, for it would reveal the sort of work he had done with these young men during the three years of their training.

Daniel and his friends had nothing to fear, however, as they well knew. In fact, the text makes clear that when the examination was over, they were found to be the best of all the group. Nebuchadnezzar "found none like" these four. This is most significant, for the other young men were all high-quality teen-agers as well. But Daniel and his friends were the "top four" at graduation. And, as a result, "they stood before the king." The meaning of the phrase here is the same as in verse 5: they were given positions of service. Since certainly the other young men were also given positions, the thought must be that these received the higher positions. These are not described here but in Daniel 2:48, 49, as will be seen.

The evaluation of the four given in verse 20 seems to refer not only to the day of graduation but also to days following, after their respective positions had been assigned. "In all matters of wisdom and understanding," they were found to be "ten times better" than any others in similar positions in all the king's realm. This must have been very gratifying to the four. When they had made their decision of three years before, it had seemed that they might finish last. Still, they had put God's will first in their decision; and now God had honored them in it by this most significant result. Their choice had indeed been right, and these results now made all the ridicule and scoffing they had experienced more than worthwhile. They now enjoyed the finest positions of all the group, and no more jeers and taunts would be heard. How good God is! How worthwhile to obey Him all the way!

The closing verse states that Daniel continued to live and serve through all the years of the Babylonian empire until the reign of Cyrus, who brought that empire to an end. Contrary to the way matters had looked in Daniel's earliest days in Babylon when it seemed that he might not last even the three years of training, he did indeed last and even continued until Babylon itself had passed. That Daniel did not speak of himself continuing into the reign of Cyrus a few years — which he did (see Dan. 10:1) — may indicate that he wrote at least this part of the book in the first year of Cyrus. He could not have known then, of course, just how much longer God would permit him to live. But at least God had continued his life all the time of the Babylonian period, long after Nebuchadnezzar himself — and probably all the others involved at this early graduation time — had died. Though storms of intrigue had passed over him, with opposition having been severe, no doubt almost continually, he had survived and outlived them all because of God's grace.

For Further Study

1. Read articles in a Bible dictionary or encyclopedia on: (a) Jehoiakim, (b) food.
2. Describe the character of the king of Judah at the time Daniel was taken captive.
3. What were the Hebrew names of Daniel's three friends? What Babylonian names were given to all four?
4. Why would the four have been defiled if they had eaten the king's menu?
5. List attractions which the four had to face in asking for a substitute menu.
6. How did a good reputation help Daniel at this time?
7. Characterize how the four must have felt when they graduated at the head of the class.
8. What do you see as the main lesson to learn from this chapter?

Chapter 2

Nebuchadnezzar's Dream Interpreted

Chapter 2 concerns a dream Nebuchadnezzar had. The dream occurred early in Daniel's experience in Babylon, even before the close of his training period. The dream is significant for picturing history through four successive Gentile empires, the last of which, in a reconstituted form, will continue even into the last days of the world. The dream finally depicts the rise of Christ's millennial kingdom and its complete destruction of that restored empire.

A. Nebuchadnezzar's Disturbing Dream (Dan. 2:1-13)

Nebuchadnezzar used this dream as a way of testing the authenticity of Babylon's wise men. The king wanted the dream interpreted and, according to custom, called these men for the purpose. Departing from custom, however, he did not tell them the content of the dream, but insisted they tell him this, as well as the interpretation, to prove the reliability of the interpretation. They could not meet the test, and this provided an opportunity for Daniel to present God's true interpretation.

1. The dream (Dan. 2:1)

God used various methods by which to reveal information in Bible times, but the method He used with pagans was the dream. The probable reason is that a dream was the most appropriate in their case, for it imparted information when the person was neutralized by sleep, so that he could not make a wrong manner of response while the revelation was being given. Dreams were given, for instance, to Abimelech, king of Gerar (Gen. 20:3), to Pharaoh in Joseph's time (Gen. 41), and to others, as well as here to Nebuchadnezzar.

Nebuchadnezzar's dream occurred in the second year of his reign. By this time Daniel was about half finished with his three years of training,[1] and was perhaps sixteen or seventeen years old. Nebuchadnezzar was severely disturbed by the dream, not being able to return to sleep that night. Recognizing the significance of the dream, he immediately called for the wise men of his country to come and interpret it for him.

2. The arrival of the wise men (Dan. 2:2-4)

It may be assumed that the wise men came as soon as the king gave the order, though the time may have been early the following morning. These men are designated by four terms, perhaps best translated as "magicians, enchanters, sorcerers, and chaldeans." Wise men are mentioned several times in the book of Daniel, and a total of six terms are used to describe them with usually a different number and combination of terms being used each time. This reflects the fact that they were composed of various groups, each group having an area of specialty. (This is known also from secular sources.) The fact that the terms are used in different combinations, however, suggests that they are not used precisely to indicate these particular specialty areas but rather generally as a way of indicating all the wise men as a group. Such men were highly honored in ancient society and were important members of the priesthood. They exercised great influence in a kingdom, because their advice was regularly sought before major decisions were made or actions taken.

On arriving before Nebuchadnezzar in this instance the wise men responded with confidence that, if the king would tell them his dream, they would gladly indicate its interpretation. They could have given an interpretation, too, for dream-interpretation was a common way of revealing the will of their deities. It no doubt would not have been the correct interpretation, for they had only their books and formulas by which to make it, but they would have thought it was correct.

The insertion of the phrase "in Syriac" or, better, "in Aramaic," is to say not only that these men responded to Nebuchadnezzar in

---

[1]Because Daniel received appointment to office as a result of interpreting this dream (Dan. 2:48), some expositors believe that this occasion must have followed the training period. To make the time work out right on this basis, the three years of training are taken as lasting only one full year plus parts of a preceding and a succeeding year, thus reducing it to perhaps as little as fourteen months. In this context, however, it is preferable to take the time as three full years and see the appointment of Daniel as taking effect at the close of this time, with only the designation being made earlier.

Aramaic, but that the book of Daniel uses Aramaic as its language from this point on till the close of chapter 7 (see Introduction).

3. *An unexpected demand (Dan. 2:5-13)*

At this point, Nebuchadnezzar astonished and dismayed these proud men by refusing to tell them his dream. It should be observed that the phrase in verses 5 and 8 (KJV), "is gone from me," meaning that Nebuchadnezzar had forgotten the dream is the translation of an Aramaic word best taken to mean "is made sure."[2] The continuing story also implies that the king had not forgotten the dream but rather wanted to test the ability and veracity of these men. In fact, he stated this directly in verse 9: "Tell me the dream, and I shall know that you can show me the interpretation." "The thing is gone from me," then, can better be translated, "The order from me is sure," meaning that his warning of punishment for the wise men was sure to be carried out if they failed to fulfill his demand.

The king gave both positive and negative incentives for the wise men to do as he asked. If they did not, they would be "cut in pieces" and their houses "made a dunghill." This meant they would lose both life and property. If they met the requirement, however, they would receive "gifts and rewards and great honour." The positive incentives were as attractive as the negative ones were repulsive.

Though the incentives were strong, the wise men still could not comply. They had no way of knowing what the king had dreamed. Twice they responded (vv. 7, 10, 11) that they would gladly give the interpretation, but they could not tell the dream. They went so far as to actually rebuke the king when they stated in their second response that no other king had ever made such a demand, implying that Nebuchadnezzar was really out of place in doing so. What they said was quite true, for the normal thing was for kings to accept the interpretations of the wise men without question. These men did not help their case with Nebuchadnezzar, however, by making the statement. They also said that such information lay solely with "the gods," implying again that Nebuchadnezzar was unreasonable in asking mortal men to supply it. Though these statements did not help their own situation, the words did serve to prepare matters nicely for Daniel's entrance on the scene, when he indeed was able

---

[2]The KJV rendition, following Greek and Latin versions, seems to find the root of the Aramaic word in *'azal,* meaning "to go away or depart." This root is very unlikely, however, for it involves a substitution of a "d" for an "l." The root is better taken as a Persian loan word, best translated here as "sure."

to give the information, which had been imparted by the true God of heaven.

The result of the inability of the wise men was that Nebuchadnezzar became exceedingly angry and ordered their death. He included in the order "all the wise men of Babylon," whether present or not, and among these were numbered Daniel and his three friends, though they were only in training at the time. Therefore, the four were soon sought to be assembled for execution, along with the many others.

B. The Dream Revealed to Daniel (Dan. 2:14-30)

Though the resulting visit by a squad of executioners would have been a terrifying experience for these young men, it was God's way of permitting Daniel an entrance before Nebuchadnezzar, that he might give the mighty king God's intended interpretation.

1. *Daniel's promise to Nebuchadnezzar (Dan. 2:14-16)*

Daniel's poise as a teen-ager before the group of executioners when they arrived is most noteworthy. The squad included the captain of the whole operation, Arioch. That he was with the group made the visit even more frightening, but it also made Daniel's request to see the king possible. If only lesser men had come, none would have been able to arrange such a meeting. The appearance of such a group would have made most people cringe in terror, but not Daniel. No doubt of strong personality by nature, and especially enabled by God here, he asked Arioch, "Why is the decree so hasty from the king?" Amazingly, this man of authority answered Daniel's query. This is really surprising. Arioch surely was a rough and rugged person, holding the position he did, and he must have been accustomed to people trying to "beg off" from deserved punishment. One has to wonder why such a man was willing to respond in this way to Daniel. The full answer, of course, can only be found in God's special intervention, but it may be assumed that He employed Daniel's own bearing and courage as a means. Arioch, too, may have known of this young man's fine reputation, even as Ashpenaz and the melzar did, and therefore he would be inclined to be patient with him.

At this point in the text (between verses 15 and 16), a bit of conversation between Daniel and Arioch must be imagined. Daniel must have requested the meeting with the king described in verse 16.

This would have involved his assertion that he would be able to meet the king's demand, and this, in turn, would have called for a testimony again to the reality and power of his God. It required, further, that Arioch be sufficiently impressed with these words for him to make an appointment for Daniel with Nebuchadnezzar and for the king to be willing to grant it.

Daniel's appearance before Nebuchadnezzar must have been a memorable experience for him. He can be imagined dressing in his finest for the occasion, no doubt with the anxious help of his three friends. Much discussion would have ensued as to how to act properly before such a monarch. But finally the hour came for Daniel to go; we can see him moving out of his residence hall, down the street to the palace, and then ushered in before the most powerful king in the world. The scene that greeted him must have been resplendent, with guards and attendants at hand, and plush rugs and tapestries adorning the room. Just to stand before such a ruler would be a nerve-racking experience, making most people want to be anywhere but there.

Daniel, however, did not waver in his intention. He voiced the words that he had prepared. He requested that he be given some time so that he might learn and then bring back to the king the information the king desired. This took great courage and faith on Daniel's part, for by this request he was promising to do what the honored wise men, all much older than he, had failed to do. He had no idea at the time what the king had dreamed, but still he promised the king that he would return with that information at the time the king would set. Few men have ever demonstrated faith like this, much less a youth still in his teens.

2. A teen-agers' prayer meeting (Dan. 2:17, 18)

The result of Daniel's promise to the king was a remarkable teen-agers' prayer meeting. Daniel returned to his friends back in the residence hall and told them what had happened. Then he urged that together they "desire mercies of the God of heaven concerning this secret" of the king's dream. He wanted all four to pray unitedly that God would reveal the information they needed. It should be noticed that Daniel laid stress on desiring "mercies" from God. He clearly recognized that God in no way owed this revelation to the four, and that, if God was pleased to grant it, it would only be on the basis of His mercy. So, then, the burden of their prayer was on asking God for mercy. They had to present the kind of humble, repentant heart that would allow God to respond in this way. In this Daniel showed his own recognition that God is willing to grant favor to His people, provided their hearts are prepared to receive it.

With this report and instruction given, Daniel and the three can be imagined bowing on bended knees in a circle of prayer. This is a significant picture to fix in mind: four teen-agers on their knees before God in a prayer meeting. And how earnest must have been their petition! They needed to have this information from God, or else Daniel would not be able to fulfill his promise to the king, and they would all lose their lives, along with many others. Sometimes people think that young people cannot really pray, but they can. Daniel and his friends surely did here. God is ready to hear all who come in faith.

3. *The prayer answered (Dan. 2:19-23)*

No indication is given as to how long the four prayed before they ceased, but it is clear that God did not answer them during the actual prayer time. The text says that the answer came "in a night vision" to Daniel. But, whether sooner or later, it did come, and the fact must have been as stirring and thrilling to Daniel as anything could possibly be. God really told him what Nebuchadnezzar had dreamed! Since this was the first of such revelations to Daniel, it would have been the more impressive. How much Daniel may have slept after going to bed, it is not possible to say, but it is all but certain that he did not sleep at all after receiving the vision; there was too much to do and talk about. We can imagine him waking the other three quickly from their sleep and telling them the good news, no doubt relating the full dream to them.

Then the four had another prayer meeting, this time to give thanks. Daniel led in this prayer, and the words are recorded in verses 20-23. Interestingly, God prompted Daniel, in later writing his book, to record the words of this prayer, when he did not record the prayer of request. The significance may be that God is more interested in praise than in request (though surely He is not uninterested in the latter, as many passages make clear). It is true, however, that Christians tend to be much shorter in their praise than in their requests. Daniel was not short in his praise at this time. In fact, the prayer he voiced at this night hour is made up only of praise, with not so much as one word of request included. In this it is highly unique.

In verses 20-22 of the prayer, Daniel praised God generally, speaking of His power and wisdom. He said God is characterized by "wisdom and might"; then he enlarged on this thought by citing four examples: God changes times and seasons through His control of history; one way He does this is by removing and establishing kings; He gives wisdom and knowledge where He sees it to be needed (as Daniel had just received, and as Christians are promised in James 1:5); and He reveals information not known or knowable in any other way, for He knows what is "in the darkness." Further, in verse 23, Daniel expressed praise for God's answer in Daniel's specific need regarding "the king's matter." Daniel, thus, gave praise to God in both a general and specific manner, and in this he provided a fine example. Christians of any day are to do the same (see Luke 17:11-18).

4. *The return to Nebuchadnezzar (Dan. 2:24-26)*

Daniel quickly made arrangements through Arioch to see the king again. Though a set time for reporting to the king had probably been made, still an appointment apparently was necessary; or, it may be that Daniel wanted to see the king earlier than the time set. Notice that Daniel's first statement was in behalf of the other wise men. He might have taken an "I told you so" attitude, stating that he now had the information the king wanted, but the text gives his first words as, "Destroy not the wise men of Babylon." His first thoughts were for others, rather than on what he was able to do. How commendable this action was!

Daniel also conveyed the information that he could now tell the king what he wanted to know; then Arioch made the necessary arrangements. He personally escorted Daniel to the king this time and sought some honor for himself by claiming to have found one who could "make known unto the king the interpretation." Men regularly seek glory for themselves, and Arioch did here. He really had not found Daniel at all, but he claimed the honor. It is true that he deserved some credit, for he had not turned Daniel away from seeing the king, and he had also arranged the two appointments. But this is all he had done.

Nebuchadnezzar's first remark was to inquire of Daniel as to the accuracy of Arioch's statement. Could Daniel really tell the dream and its interpretation? It was hard for the king to believe that this was possible when the veteran wise men had failed completely.

5. *Daniel's significant response to Nebuchadnezzar (Dan. 2:27-30)*

Daniel's reply deserves the highest commendation. Here he was back before the king, with all that awesome atmosphere, this time with the desired information in hand. How easy it would have been to boast a little and seek glory for himself. But he did not do this. Rather, he made a definite point of telling the king that the information he was about to set forth was not because of any wisdom he had, but solely because the true God of heaven had revealed it to him.

Note especially Daniel's words to Nebuchadnezzar in verse 28: "But there is a God in heaven that revealeth secrets"; and then in verse 30, "But as for me, this secret is not revealed to me for any wisdom that I have." Daniel began his reply in verse 27 by referring to the inability of the Babylonian wise men shown earlier; he made this reference to show the superiority of the true God of heaven. These men who had failed worshiped the Babylonian gods, but he, Daniel, who now would tell the king all he wanted to know, worshiped the true God. This was a forceful testimony to this pagan monarch, and it took great courage to make it, but Daniel did not hesitate. He was about to tell this ruler what he had dreamed, along with the meaning, and he wanted him to understand without mistake how this was possible.

In verse 29 Daniel included one other thought. It concerned the general meaning of the dream as a sort of introductory note. He stated that the dream was intended by God to symbolize what would come to pass in the future. The first words of the verse indicate that Nebuchadnezzar had been wondering about this very matter as he lay in bed that night, and Daniel wanted him to know that God had answered him through the dream.

C. The Dream and Its Interpretation (Dan. 2:31-45)

With this preliminary explanation, Daniel began to give the information that was so important to the king. He first told the dream itself, giving proof of the authenticity of his interpretation, and then he moved on to that interpretation, which carried the main significance.

1. *The dream itself (Dan. 2:31-35)*

Daniel first told the king that his dream concerned an image; then he proceeded to describe it generally. He said it was "great" (meaning especially that it was large, though the size is not given), bright (apparently from its shining metal construction), standing upright (thus apparently human in appearance), and "terrible" (meaning awesome).

Then Daniel became more specific. He noted the four different metals from which the image was made. Its head was of gold, its breast and arms of silver, its belly and thighs of brass, its legs of iron and feet of iron and baked clay mixed. It should be observed that the word for "clay" is definitely "baked clay," which is brittle, and not soft, natural clay. The feet of the image, then, were entirely hard; but the iron part was hard and strong, while the clay part was hard and brittle. Then Daniel stated that the king saw a stone "cut out without hands," which struck the image at its feet, so that the image fell and was completely shattered. The pieces were so fine that the wind was able to blow them away like chaff. Then the destroying stone became large and "filled the whole earth."

2. The dream interpreted (Dan. 2:36-45)

With the dream given, Daniel proceeded with the interpretation, the king being ready to receive it since the dream had been told exactly as he had seen it.

a. The four empires of ancient time (Dan. 2:36-41). The interpretation Daniel gave concerned four world empires that were to succeed each other in future history. In verses 37 and 38 he said that the head of gold symbolized Nebuchadnezzar as head of the Babylonian Empire. Because gold is the most valuable metal and because it constituted the head of the image, Babylonia, as led by Nebuchadnezzar, obviously was the leading empire of the four represented. This was true, not because of size (for actually it was the smallest in this respect), but because of strength of organization and especially because it had as king Nebuchadnezzar, one of the most capable rulers of ancient history. Daniel made clear that this glorious kingdom had been given to Nebuchadnezzar by "the God of heaven," the same God who had revealed this dream to Daniel.

Daniel was brief in his description of the following two empires. The second, symbolized by silver, can clearly be identified with Medo-Persia, which, we know from history, did supplant Babylonia. Cyrus the Great established it, as he first united Media and Persia and then conquered an enormous amount of land stretching from the Aegean Sea to India. Daniel called it "inferior," but this does not refer to its size; it concerns, rather, its strength of organization and leadership.

From history again, the third empire, represented by brass, is known to be Greece. Daniel said this kingdom would "bear rule over all the earth"; the vast territory which Alexander the Great amassed for Greece was even larger than Medo-Persia. Alexander caused this empire to supplant that of Medo-Persia, just as the image symbolized.

The fourth empire was given much more attention by Daniel. He said it would be characterized especially by strength, as symbolized by iron. As iron is strong enough to break all the previous metals, so this empire would be able to do away with all the preceding empires. Actually, it only had to replace the Grecian empire, but since each previous empire had replaced its predecessor, the final empire did in a real sense replace or destroy the first three. This empire, as known again from history, was Rome, which continued in power from 146 B.C., the date of the fall of Corinth, to A.D. 476, when Rome fell to the barbaric hordes of Europe. It survived longer than the earlier three empires put together (they had endured from 605 to 146 B.C.), thus showing true durative strength, like iron.

The words of verse 41, however, show an inner weakness of Rome. In its feet and toes, the image was partly iron (strong) and partly baked clay (weak). Because this mixture existed only in the feet and not in the legs, the symbolism is that this condition would arise in Rome's later stages. The iron should be understood to symbolize Rome's strength in governmental organization, which continued to make Rome strong for all of its history. The fragile baked clay is best taken in reference to the weakness in moral fiber that developed among the people in Rome's later days. They came to love pleasure, dissipation, and luxurious living, and this, working against the strength of the governmental organization, served to bring about its downfall.

b. The restored Roman empire of future time (Dan. 2:42, 43).
At some point in this symbolism an extended gap in time must be fixed, because by verse 44 the interpretation describes the future day of Christ's millennial reign, as will be seen. The best point at which to see that gap is between verses 41 and 42. For one thing, in verse 42 the toes of the image are stressed, with no mention of either legs or feet any longer. These toes logically correspond to the ten horns of the fourth beast of Daniel's first vision, set forth in Daniel 7:7. This beast is parallel in its symbolism to the legs and feet of Nebuchadnezzar's dream. The horns there are specifically identified with "ten kings" (Dan. 7:24), which implies that these ten toes carry the

same symbolism. But at no time in ancient history did Rome have ten contemporaneous kings, though this image had ten toes all at the same time. Therefore, a restored form of the empire will have to come to existence, when this situation will occur. It is true that "toes" are mentioned in verse 41 already, but there the reference is only along with "feet" and should probably be understood to indicate that the same basic empire, only in restored form, is meant in the following verse.

Since the toes of verses 42 and 43 are said to be mixed (inter-mingled) in their make-up of iron and baked clay, the restored empire will evidently have strong and weak elements, like the ancient empire. This time, however, the language is different, as it speaks of the iron and clay being "mixed," or better, "intermingled," but still not cleaving to one another. The meaning of the symbolism of verse 41 does not fit this language. These verses are best taken to refer either to an intermingling of strong people from strong countries with weak people from weak countries, or else stronger people within a given country with weaker people of that country, to provide overall strength. That the two aspects do not cleave, however, shows that the effort to achieve greater strength will not prove successful. So, then, the future kingdom will have its internal problems, just like all kingdoms before it, making for weakness within.

   c. Christ's millennial kingdom (Dan. 2:44, 45). Daniel next showed the significance of the stone which Nebuchadnezzar saw destroying the great image. He stated that it symbolized a kingdom set up by God, in contrast to the earlier four, which were set up by men. That the stone strikes the image at its feet means that this kingdom will strike and destroy the fourth empire in its last stage, when the toes are in view, which means at the time of its restoration. This is in keeping with the thought that this kingdom is truly the kingdom of Christ of the millennial age. Several other matters also give evidence to this thought and call for notice.

For one thing, this kingdom is established by God; it is symbol-ized by a stone "cut out of the mountain *without hands*" (v. 45). The human hands of earthly kings shaped the earlier empires, but this one will be formed by God supernaturally. Further, this kingdom cannot be a spiritual kingdom, established by Christ at His first coming (as some expositors believe), because the stone smites the image at its feet, including the toes, and they symbolize the kingdom's last point in history, when ten contemporary kings will rule. But

Christ came the first time when the Roman empire had just started and surely not when ten contemporary kings were in power. Third, the rise of this new kingdom will be sudden, indicated by the complete destruction of the image at one blow of the stone. The Roman Empire, however, was not crushed by Christ's first coming. Indeed, the empire came to its greatest strength after that coming, and it was never crushed by the early church which was started as a result of that coming. In contrast, when Christ comes the second time, it will be to the Mount of Olives (Zech. 14:4), where He will utterly destroy in a moment the Gentile armies assembled there, and then, shortly after, He will establish His millennial kingdom. Fourth, the new kingdom will grow to fill all the earth, as did the stone of the dream (Dan. 2:35). But the church, started by Christ at His first coming, has never become dominant in the earth. In fact, today the number of people becoming true followers of Christ continues to fall further and further behind the growth of population. Christ's millennial kingdom, however, will truly fill all the earth (Ps. 2:6-9); He will rule over all the world, with His capital at Jerusalem. Fifth, the fact that this kingdom is parallel in the dream to the four earlier kingdoms implies that this one will also be physical and earthly in type, just as they were, and not spiritual.

In this symbolism the stress is on the durative strength of this kingdom, as established by God. It is able to break all prior kingdoms, as the stone broke the image, and then is able to "stand forever." In contrast to all the previous empires, which were destroyed in due time, God's kingdom will not come to such an end.

3. *Daniel honored (Dan. 2:45-49)*

The concluding section of the chapter concerns Nebuchadnezzar's response to these significant words of Daniel. He highly honored the young man and praised the God to whom Daniel had given all credit. He actually bowed before Daniel and rendered worship, calling for offerings and sweet odors (incense) to be extended to him. This was an incredible action by an emperor — bowing before a mere captive! What changes God can effect in man's heart. It is doubtful, however, that Nebuchadnezzar thought of Daniel himself as God. At the beginning, Daniel had clearly pointed out that his information was not of himself, but of the God of heaven. Nebuchadnezzar was only seeking to worship this God through Daniel.

This thought is borne out further by the king's words: "Of a truth it is, that your God is a God of gods, and a Lord of kings." By this remarkable statement, Nebuchadnezzar was really admitting that Daniel's God was greater than the gods of Babylon. In the Introduction, it was pointed out that one of Daniel's contributions was in maintaining God's honor in the Babylonian palace. This was the first instance of his doing so, and it was a striking one.

Verse 48 indicates that Nebuchadnezzar then gave Daniel not one but actually two high positions in the government. After bestowing "many great gifts" (cf. Dan. 2:6), he first made Daniel "ruler over the whole province of Babylon." The empire was divided into several provinces, each with a governor. The most important province was where the capital was located, called the province of Babylon. Daniel was made governor of this province, which was surely a high honor. Second, Daniel was made "chief of the governors over all the wise men of Babylon." Daniel had shown himself superior to the other wise men, and now the king suited his future role to this superiority. Though the first position was an important honor, this second one was still more important. In this position Daniel would have frequent and significant contact with the mighty king, and could wield strong influence. How gratifying this manner of reward must have been to Daniel, when it had seemed just a few months before that neither he nor his friends would obtain any position at all. God had truly been faithful.

Then verse 49 indicates that Daniel did not forget his three friends, who had been through the hardship of that earlier day with him. Having received his own reward, he now spoke in their behalf, and the king appointed the three "over the affairs of the province of Babylon." The thought is probably that they were made Daniel's assistants in conducting the business of one of his positions. He may have asked specifically that they be given these places, since he would have wanted them near him, and because they would be valuable and trustworthy. In fact, because of the concluding statement, "but Daniel sat in the gate of the king," it may be that he virtually turned the operation of the province over to them. His task as head of the wise men was enough to keep him busy. That he sat "in the gate of the king" means that his office was in the place of the king's own business. Ancient gates were considered appropriate places for judges and officers to conduct official business (see Deut. 16:18; Ruth 4:1-12; Esther 3:2). Because gates were used in this way, they came in time to give their name to the royal offices (palace) of the king, which is the likely meaning here.

All four young men, then, finally held the high positions they had dared hope for from the first but had believed lost when they made their decision to refuse the king's menu. That God worked matters out so they did receive the positions after all is one of the fine examples of how God honors those who honor Him.

For Further Study

1. Read articles in a Bible dictionary or encyclopedia on: (a) dream, (b) Persia, (c) Greece, (d) Roman Empire.
2. What was unusual about the demand Nebuchadnezzar made of the wise men? Why did he make it?
3. How was it that the king's death decree came to the attention of Daniel?
4. What did Daniel promise Nebuchadnezzar?
5. What did Daniel make clear to Nebuchadnezzar before he told him the dream? Why was this important?
6. Describe the image seen in the dream and tell what each part symbolized.
7. What did the ten toes symbolize?
8. What did the great stone smiting the image on the feet symbolize?
9. What two high positions was Daniel given as a reward for giving the interpretation?

DANIEL'S PROPHECIES AT A GLANCE

	Babylon (605-538 B.C.)	Medo-Persia (538-331 B.C.)	Greece (331-146 B.C.)	Rome (146 B.C.—A.D. 500)	(PRESENT-AGE GAP OF MANY CENTURIES)	Last Days (still future)
Daniel 2:31-45 Dream Image (603 B.C.)	Head of gold (2:32, 37, 38)	Breast, arms of silver (2:32, 39)	Belly, thighs of brass (2:32, 39)	Legs of iron Feet of iron and clay (2:33, 40, 41)		Toes of iron and clay (2:33, 42, 43) Stone cut without hands (2:34, 35, 44, 45)
Daniel 7 First vision: Four beasts (553 B.C.)	Lion (7:4)	Bear (7:5)	Leopard (7:6)	Strong Beast (7:7, 11, 19, 23)		Ten horns (7:7, 20, 24) Little horn (7:8, 20, 21, 24-26) Reign of Christ (7:13, 14, 18, 22, 27)
Daniel 8 Second vision: Ram and goat (551 B.C.)		Ram (8:3, 4, 10)	Goat with one horn (8:5-8, 21) Four horns (8:8, 22) Little horn (8:9-14)			Roman "Beast" prefigured by little horn (8:23-25)
Daniel 9:24-27 Third vision: 70 weeks (538 B.C.)		From commandment going forth— Ezra, 458 B.C. (9:25)	69 weeks continue (9:25)	Until Messiah be cut off—A.D. 26 (9:26)		70th week of Tribulation (9:27)
Daniel 10-12 Fourth vision: Tribulation period (536 B.C.)		Four kings (11:2)	Mighty King and kingdom divided (11:3, 4) Kings of north and south (11:5-20) Vile king, Antiochus Epiphanes			Roman "Beast," Antichrist (11:36-45) Tribulation and its chronology (12:1-13)

Chapter 3

Standing Tall in Spite of a Fiery Furnace

The story of chapter 3 involves only Daniel's three friends and not Daniel himself. Perhaps Daniel was ill, or he may have been out of the country on business for the king; at least only Shadrach, Meshach, and Abed-nego appear in the account. They have been mentioned in a secondary role in the previous two chapters, and after this chapter they do not appear at all. In this chapter, however, they are the central figures. Apparently God directed Daniel to include this story to let readers know that they were also of sterling quality, along with Daniel.

The time of the episode is not stated. It was at least after the three years of training, because the three are here depicted as active officers in the land, no doubt in the positions assigned at the end of chapter 2. Evidence can be presented, too, that it occurred not long after they had assumed those posts. Nebuchadnezzar here commanded all his official family to bow before a great statue, which quite clearly represented the gods of Babylonia. Because he had a fiery furnace made ready for all who might disobey, he apparently believed that some might. It would appear, then, that he was testing the loyalty of his officers to the Babylonian religious system; it is likely that he would have done such a thing earlier in his reign rather than later. He would have wanted to know soon where each official stood. Perhaps, then, not more than two years or so had elapsed since the three years of training, which would make the young men about twenty years old.

A. Nebuchadnezzar's Order (Dan. 3:1-7)

1. *The image (Dan. 3:1)*

The chapter begins with the indication that Nebuchadnezzar made a great image and commanded that all his official family bow before it. The command brought another crucial time of decision for Shadrach, Meshach, and Abed-nego.

Perhaps the idea for making this statue was suggested by the dream Nebuchadnezzar had seen in chapter 2. The statue was immense — sixty cubits high (ninety feet) and six cubits wide (nine feet). Since this ratio of width to height is one to ten, and the normal ratio for a person is about one to five, it is likely that the ninety feet included a sizable base. Made of gold (hardly solid, but probably gold plated over a wooden frame), it was extremely valuable. It was located in the "plain of Dura," probably best identified with Tolul Dura (mounds of Dura), not far from ancient Babylon. On one of the mounds there, archeologist Julius Oppert found an actual large brick square, forty-five feet on a side and twenty feet high, which he suggests was the foundation of this image. The statue certainly was intended to represent the gods of Babylon, because everyone was commanded to fall down and worship it.

2. The assembly for dedication (Dan. 3:2, 3)

With the statue erected, Nebuchadnezzar gave orders for its proper dedication. In keeping with the size and value of the image, the dedication called for the assembly of all Nebuchadnezzar's officers from all parts of his empire; they were ordered to attend. The list of these officers in verse 2 places them in a descending order of rank, from the "princes" ("satraps" as they were then called, who, like Daniel, were the heads of provinces) down to the "sheriffs" (minor judicial officials), besides "all the rulers," meaning everyone else not listed but still holding an official position. Apparently, Nebuchadnezzar wanted to test the loyalty of everyone, even if it meant leaving the affairs of government in the hands of minor subordinates for a time. It should be recognized that a matter of days would have been involved in getting messages out to all the distant points and for the officers to make the trip to Babylon.

Among those summoned to the dedication were Shadrach, Meshach, and Abed-nego. Finally the important day arrived, and we can imagine them all moving out to the site of the statue, where it stood tall and glittering against the sky. Probably strict decorum was observed, so that the highest ranking officials were given positions in the first rows and the lowest in the last. Evidently all remained standing, in view of the order soon given that all bow. With the entire official family of the empire present, the total number would have been very large, probably a few hundred at least. Each one may be imagined, dressed in his appropriate uniform, all clean and shining on this important day, to show his respective rank.

3. *The ominous message of the king's herald (Dan. 3:4-6)*

When all were in their proper places, proceedings got under way. These were begun by an announcement from the official herald of the occasion. Dressed in suitable finery, he no doubt mounted a prepared platform to issue the king's order. He declared that all assembled should do proper obeisance to the great statue by bowing before it, and that this should be done when the official orchestra began to play. It may be assumed that this orchestra was also grand, finely dressed for the occasion, in keeping with all the other aspects. The announcer continued by saying that should anyone fail to bow, he would be cast immediately into a "burning fiery furnace," which evidently was visible as he spoke.

At this point, it is well to bring to mind the effect this announcement would have had on the three friends, standing there among the assembled host. Being assistants to Daniel would have put them in the rows of second rank, meaning that most of the assembled throng was behind them. Having been ordered to take positions before the giant statue, they may have wondered, as they found their places, if just such an announcement as this might be forthcoming. They must certainly have hoped it would not, but with the official word having been proclaimed, the reality of what it meant descended on them like a cloud. They would have to make a decision as to what to do, and it would have to be made quickly. To bow before this statue would be to give open acknowledgment of obeisance to the Babylonian religious system. It would destroy the effect of all they had said and done before, during their years of refusing the king's diet, in giving witness to their faith in the true God. But it would not be easy to remain standing when everyone else bowed. Besides this, there was the terrible burning furnace. The thought of being thrown into it would have been terrifying. And they did not have long to make up their minds.

That Nebuchadnezzar had the fiery furnace ready and had the herald make special reference to it in his official announcement shows that the king feared some of his officers might refuse to bow. Probably those especially in mind were the new appointees from the recently graduated young men brought from other countries and religious backgrounds. In fact, one of the original purposes for the whole occasion may have been especially to test these foreign recruits. Were they all truly loyal Babylonians? An indirect assent had been given by them (apparently by all but the four) through the king's menu, but now they had to be tested in this more direct manner, when all would be required to bow in outright allegiance. Nebuchad-nezzar probably had all the trainees in mind, but the ones primarily affected by the order were the three young men of Judah. Whether Nebuchadnezzar realized this at all is not indicated.

4. *A general compliance (Dan. 3:7)*

Verse 7 gives the result of the herald's order. When the music began to play, everyone did bow. An entire sea of bending backs presented itself before the towering statue. In the midst of that sea, however, were three exceptions, and they must have stood out most pointedly. Shadrach, Meshach, and Abed-nego remained standing, no matter the pressure and no matter the punishment.

B. Outstanding Courage (Dan. 3:8-18)

Seldom has history witnessed greater courage than was here demonstrated by these faithful friends of Daniel. Before this, they had been able to depend on him for direction, but now they had to decide solely for themselves, and they did so with the same kind of courageous faith that characterized him.

1. *The three remained standing (Dan. 3:8)*

Actually the fact that the three remained standing is not stated directly, but the story implies it clearly enough. The story itself tells only of ready reporters going quickly to the king to give information regarding the three. These reporters may actually have been a few of the former trainees, earlier fellow-students of Shadrach, Meshach, and Abed-nego. Because the three, along with Daniel, had been different from the others during the three-year training period, and because at the close they had received the highest honors, it follows that suspicions and jealousies would have resulted. And such attitudes would not have dissipated greatly during a few intervening months. It may well be, in fact, that as the announcement of the herald was given, these former associates (who would likely have been in back of the three, having lesser appointments) kept a purposeful eye on the three, to see what they would do. They knew of their stand of past days, and they could suspect that they would not bow before this statue. If the three did not bow, then this would give the others just the reason they needed to bring discredit on them, so that they would not only be put out of their choice jobs but would lose their lives as well.

In passing, it should be observed that the three friends would have been quite aware of this sort of feeling. And this awareness could have been a contributing factor in making their decision all the more difficult, because, by not bowing, they would be playing directly into the hands of those who wished them hurt. It would have been tempting to fool these jealous enemies and actually bow. But still they knew they could not do this, not even to upset the hopes of these men, not even to protect their own jobs which they surely treasured highly, and not even to escape a terrible fiery furnace; because to bow would be to destroy all the testimony they had given until this time. They who had declared that their God was supreme and could deliver them out of any difficulty would thus be showing that they really did not believe this after all. They could not bow, and, therefore, they did not bow. They remained standing, bold against the sky, while all about bent low in the commanded obeisance. Probably one could not feel more conspicuous than did those three in the few moments of time involved. They displayed courage of the highest degree.

2. The report of the spies (Dan. 3:8-12)

The watching spies did see just what they wanted. The three Judeans did continue to stand, while all others bowed. Interestingly, the fact that these reporters were able to see the three means that they did not bow very well themselves. They would have had to twist or raise their heads in some manner, so as to be able to look in the direction of the three. As soon as the signal was given for all to stand upright once more, they were off to report to the king. Shadrach, Meshach, and Abed-nego very likely saw them go and could guess their intentions. They would have seen them come up to the king and then point in their direction. They would have seen the king rise quickly and dispatch officers in their direction. They would have seen, understood, and waited.

Notice should be made that the spies, on coming to Nebuchadnezzar, reported the three as "Jews." Verse 8 says that they accused "the Jews"; verse 12 gives their words, "There are certain Jews. . . ." This prominent use of the term suggests that the men held this national background against the three. This fact, along with their actual use of the names "Shadrach, Meshach, and Abed-nego" (v. 12), shows that they were personally acquainted with the accused; these reporters were not just indifferent observers. That they referred to the three further as those whom Nebuchadnezzar had "set over the

affairs of the province of Babylon" supports the possibility of a jealousy motive. These Jews had been appointed to this high position in
place of these reporters, and they wanted to be rid of them — that is
the implication of these words.

The charge they brought against the three Jews was threefold: that
they did not respect the king (which was false), that they did not
serve the king's gods (which was true), and that they had not bowed
before the king's statue (which was also true).

3. The exemplary response of Shadrach, Meshach, and Abed-nego (Dan. 3:13-18)

On hearing this report, Nebuchadnezzar immediately displayed
great anger. He had put forth enormous effort to make this day as
fine as he could in every way. No expense had been spared to have
everything just right, and now here three of his officers had dared to
disobey him. He quickly summoned them.

When they arrived, no doubt after being manhandled and pushed
roughly through the crowd by the king's officers, the three stal-
warts listened as Nebuchadnezzar angrily rebuked them. What he
said had a twofold purpose: first, to ascertain if the three had really
not bowed as reported, and, second, to give them a second chance to
bow. This last is indicated especially by his words in verse 15: "Now
if ye be ready. . . ." If Nebuchadnezzar had been a little less angry,
he might not have added his closing question: "Who is that God
who shall deliver you out of my hands?" For he had well learned
from Daniel, not many months before, what God it was who could do
far more than the Babylonian deities. Perhaps the very calmness of
the three before him, instead of the expected, customary terror,
tended to make him the more furious and warped both his memory
and judgment.

The three were now expected to respond, and the words they
voiced constitute one of the most exemplary replies ever given. Their
first words, that they were "not careful to answer" the king, means
that they had no need to do so. They were not being arrogant in so
speaking; rather they were simply admitting their guilt: it was true
that they had not bowed. Nebuchadnezzar had asked whether they
were guilty or not, and this was their answer.

Then they took up the king's challenge that no God existed that
could deliver them. Whether Nebuchadnezzar was king or not, they
were not about to let such words go unanswered. With forthright
boldness, they asserted that their God was indeed able to deliver

them out of the king's hand, even from the burning, fiery furnace. The strength and courage it took to speak so plainly in this circumstance can hardly be overstated. If a person has difficulty in remaining true to God today, let him remember three young Jews in foreign Babylon, standing tall, first before a gold image and then before a mighty ruler, knowing that a blazing furnace awaited them, and yet having the courage to speak such words as these.

The next words that came from their lips, however, were even more commendable, if that is possible. The first words made a great statement of faith, but these now present a remarkable declaration of submission. And, if there is anything more rare than faith, it is submission. The thought of these words is this: "Even if our God does not find it best in His will to deliver us, we still will not serve the Babylonian gods or worship the statue." Two outstanding implications should be noted. First, the young men recognized that God's will might be different than what they would find personally pleasant, and they were willing to have it so, without complaint. Too often Christians are not willing to have God's will different from their own, and then they complain when it proves so to be. Second, the young men did not make their own obedience contingent on God's doing what was pleasing to them. They were ready to obey, whether God chose to deliver them from the furnace or not. This means that they were finding the object of their affection in God Himself, and not in what God might or might not do for them. Again, what an example they set!

C. The Miraculous Deliverance (Dan. 3:19-27)

The story now tells of God's gracious deliverance of these who stated their submission to God's will in this commendable manner. They were indeed thrown into the furnace, but God delivered them from harm, and as a result Nebuchadnezzar was brought again to confess the superiority of the God of heaven.

1. *Two impetuous orders by Nebuchadnezzar (Dan. 3:19-21)*

At this courageous response by the three, Nebuchadnezzar, seeing the response as pure insolence on their part, gave quick and drastic commands concerning them. The nature of the commands shows that he lost his sense of judgment now even more than before. He first ordered the furnace heated "seven times" hotter than normal. Servants may be imagined hurrying off quickly to apply more fuel and forced draft. Then he ordered that "the most mighty men" of his army bind the three and cast them into the furnace. This was probably done by unusually strong men of the king's bodyguard. Verse 21, which says that the three were bound while yet in their garments, signifies that the three were not permitted even to remove their fine uniforms, in which they had come that day. In other words, urgency was of primary importance.

2. *A paradoxical result (Dan. 3:22, 23)*

Having bound the young men, the mighty soldiers carried them off in their helpless condition to the furnace. The furnace obviously was not far away. On arrival, a highly paradoxical event transpired. The soldiers, for all their strength, in casting the bound men into the furnace were themselves killed by the leaping flames, while the men cast inside the furnace were not harmed in any way. Outside, where there was no fire, the soldiers flamed into burning torches; and inside, where the fire blazed, the three Jews remained in perfect condition.

It was the foolish, impetuous order of the king, in calling for the furnace to be made so hot, that cost him the lives of the three prized warriors. The furnace was simply too hot to get near, and yet these men had to go near to throw the three inside. They have to be admired for being willing to carry out the king's command, though of course they would have lost their lives anyway if they had dared to disobey. Notice also that, because of these impetuous orders, Nebuchadnezzar made the deliverance God effected for the three Jews the more noteworthy. He had intended both the increased heating of the furnace and the extra strength of the soldiers to insure that no god could possibly deliver the three insolent Jews. But when God delivered them anyway, these very measures made the fact of the deliverance more impressive to all who observed. How easily God can turn man's best efforts against Him into efforts that really work for Him.

3. *God's gracious provision (Dan. 3:24-26)*

Nebuchadnezzar must have been greatly startled and disturbed that his men had been killed, but he was even more amazed when he drew near the furnace and saw a scene he could not believe. Apparently, he had walked to the furnace, probably following after the soldiers carrying their bound loads, and had taken a seat where he could see within the furnace, no doubt thinking to find satisfaction in seeing the death of those who had dared to defy him. But what he saw was in no way gratifying. It made him rise hurriedly and ask his counselors standing by, "Did not we cast three men bound into the midst of the fire?" When they replied that this was true, he said, "Lo, I see four men loose, walking in the midst of the fire, and they have no hurt." Three things astonished him: first, the three Jews had not suffered any hurt from the flames; second, they were loose and walking about, meaning that only the confining ropes had been consumed by the king's extra-hot fire; and, third, and most significant, a fourth person was walking with them, when only three had been put inside. The king's additional statement, that the form of the fourth person was "like the Son of God," can also be rendered, "like a son of the gods." The words must be understood in the light of Nebuchadnezzar's pagan thinking. The king saw this one as a divine being, no doubt because of the miraculous element involved: three people had been put into the furnace, and now here was a fourth person walking in the fire.

Though Nebuchadnezzar's own thinking regarding this fourth person is not so significant to discuss, it is important to inquire who this one really was from the biblical point of view. Two possibilities present themselves: he was an angel of God, or he was the second person of the Godhead in another preincarnate appearance. No certain answer is possible, for not enough clues exist, but perhaps the latter is more likely. Christ had appeared in similar form to Abraham at Mamre (Gen. 18), later to Joshua as the "captain of the host of the LORD" (Josh. 5:13 – 6:5), and at various times to others. God might have delivered Shadrach, Meshach, and Abed-nego without sending such a heavenly visitor, and this would have been wonderful in itself. But God in His special grace saw fit to send this personal emissary to effect the deliverance and then to accompany the three in the middle of the fire. He thus tangibly demonstrated His presence with them in their trying hour. What a significant example this is of God's remarkable grace.

When the three had been carried off to the furnace, bound hand and foot and in the powerful arms of the strong soldiers, it had surely seemed to them that God was not going to deliver them. In their courageous answer to the king they had implied that He might not; but it may be assumed that they hoped very much that He would. It now seemed that He was not going to do so. The thought of having to be cast into the burning flames must have been terrible to contemplate. Thus, when they finally were thrown in, they must have expected the worst in the way of suffering and pain. What must have been their relief and joy when this was not experienced! Here they were among roaring flames and still feeling no hurt! Then they saw their ropes being consumed, and suddenly they were loose and able to walk within the furnace (which must have been very large). And finally, and most glorious of all, they became aware of the presence of this fourth person walking with them. God had not forsaken them after all; He had indeed delivered them and here He was right with them in the furnace. Without question, they were glad all had happened just as it had. If God had kept them from the furnace, they would not now have this privilege of walking among flames in the company of the heavenly visitor. How much better it was to go through the fire with the Lord than to have missed the fire and not enjoyed His presence!

Now Nebuchadnezzar drew near to the furnace — at least as near as the heat would permit — and called for the men to come out. That was significant, for it voiced his admission that he had lost. He had defied any god to deliver these men, and now one had. And he was man enough to admit it. Of course, he really had no choice. There the three were, alive and well, in the middle of the fire, and quite clearly enjoying the experience. Thus he summoned them, calling loudly to be heard over the roaring flames, and the three did come out. Notice his reference to the "most high God" in his summons to them; by this he implied that their God had truly won over him. Their God was the "most high God," higher than the Babylonian gods.

4. A significant inspection (Dan. 3:27)

Verse 27 gives a significant setting for the emergence of the three from the blazing furnace. Not only was the king present to witness this unbelievable sight, but also his assembled officials. These men, all high in government and holding responsible positions, saw and could later give united witness to what had occurred. The king had wanted the most influential men present when he punished the three recalcitrants; but now they served as the most authoritative witnesses to God's miracle. All the lesser officials, those who had been summoned from all parts of the empire to worship the image, would have been present, too, probably farther back but still where they could see. They would go back all across the empire, and, as they went, they would be firsthand witnesses to tell of the miracle they had seen. Nebuchadnezzar had assembled them to give praise to the gods of Babylon, but they would go home with reason only to praise the God whom Nebuchadnezzar had thought to defy.

As soon as the three young men came out of the furnace, they were inspected carefully. One can imagine all the higher officials taking advantage of their position now to draw near and inspect the three at close range. The fact that the three were yet alive was reason enough to marvel, but what the officials found made them wonder even more. Their inspection revealed that the bodies of the three had not been hurt in any way; even their hair showed no evidence of being singed. Their clothes were not burned or marked, and they did not even have the smell of fire on them. These were remarkable facts, indeed. Singed hair, or black marks of burnt carbon, or at least the smell of fire should have been present, even if no physical harm had been experienced. The officials must have been speechless in amazement as they moved back from what their inspection had revealed. They had never seen anything like this before. They would not have been speechless, however, on returning home, as they told many times over the story of what had happened that memorable day.

D. The Commendable Reaction of Nebuchadnezzar (Dan. 3:28-30)

Nebuchadnezzar and his officers, then, did indeed witness the unmistakable evidence of the supremacy of the God of heaven that day. They could not claim any use of trickery, for they had all observed everything that had transpired. Their minds had to accept the fact that the God of these Jews had been proven the highest of all. It would be pleasing to think that some of the officers went home not only to tell of the remarkable event but also to place their personal trust in this God. Nothing is indicated to this end, however; but of Nebuchadnezzar, at least, it is stated that he made some tangible acknowledgments, though certainly they fell short of personal trust.

Verses 28 and 29 give the words he spoke following the inspection, apparently while all the dignitaries were yet present. He first pronounced blessing on the God of the three young men. Then he asserted that their God had sent a heavenly messenger to deliver them because of their trust in Him. And, finally, he admitted that the three had truly "changed the king's word" (that is, frustrated his word, given so boldly a short time previously) when they had "yielded their bodies, that they might not serve nor worship any god, except their own God." This was a remarkable statement of commendation for the young men and a humiliating confession for himself. It was really quite a statement to make, especially when his chief officers were present to hear.

As a result, Nebuchadnezzar now issued a public decree that all his realm might know of the occasion. Actually, of course, the realm would learn from all the attending personnel, but the decree added a significant note of authority in support of the unofficial renditions. The thrust of the edict was that any person in his realm should "speak anything amiss" (anything erroneous) against the God of these three, he should be cut in pieces and his house be made a dunghill. Then he gave the reason: there was no God (including the Babylonian deities) who could deliver in the way he had just seen happen before his eyes. Such was the message of the decree, and this, certainly, was startling information to be made public, which everyone, including the Babylonian priests, would read. Had Nebuchadnezzar not been as powerful as he was, he would not have dared issue such a statement. But being powerful, he did, and that shows he had been greatly impressed by the occasion.

The last notice was that Shadrach, Meshach, and Abed-nego were honored with a promotion. What a change thus came for the three because of their faithfulness to God. In place of deprivation and death, which had faced them a short time earlier when they were bound and carried to the furnace, they now had an excellent promotion instead. How good their God was to them!

For Further Study

1. Read articles in a Bible dictionary or encyclopedia on: (a) Dura and (b) furnace.
2. Describe the statue built by Nebuchadnezzar.
3. Why would it have been wrong for the three friends to bow before it?
4. What two outstanding virtues characterized their manner of reply to Nebuchadnezzar?
5. Why do you believe God permitted the three friends to be cast into the furnace?
6. When Nebuchadnezzar's many officers later returned to their homes, what would have been their most impressive memory of this day of dedication?
7. What benefits did the three friends receive from Nebuchadnezzar after their deliverance from the furnace?

Chapter 4

Nebuchadnezzar's Second Dream

Chapter 4 presents Nebuchadnezzar's second dream. In the dream the king saw a large tree which was cut down at the command of a heavenly messenger. Daniel interpreted the dream for the king, stating that the tree symbolized Nebuchadnezzar and that its fall represented a seven-year period of insanity that he would suffer. The chapter tells of this condition coming on the great monarch, his restoration to sanity after seven years, and his resulting ascription of honor once more to the God of heaven.

The story does not indicate at what time during Nebuchadnezzar's reign the dream occurred, but there are clues that place it at the end of his reign. Nebuchadnezzar ruled forty-three years (605-562 B.C.), and, following his period of insanity, he was restored to his throne for at least a few months. This period of restoration does not appear to have been long, however, perhaps not more than a year. Twelve months elapsed following the dream until the beginning of the seven years of insanity (Dan. 4:29). Thus, one must add this year to the seven years of insanity, plus the approximate year of restoration to the throne, and subtract them from the total years of his reign to get the latest date in the reign for the dream. This works out to be the king's thirty-fourth year, which perhaps is the most likely date. If this is correct, then thirty-two years had elapsed since Nebuchadnezzar's first dream (which came in his second year, Dan. 2:1), and Daniel was now about forty-nine years old.

This chapter gives the third miraculous contact God made with Nebuchadnezzar. Daniel's interpretation of Nebuchadnezzar's first dream had come in the second year of his reign, the remarkable deliverance of the three friends in perhaps his fifth year, and now this in about his thirty-fourth year. Nebuchadnezzar had been significantly impressed by the first two contacts, but he was still more by this third one. He may even have come to place personal faith in the God of heaven in this instance, as will be discussed later in the chapter.

The form of this chapter is unique in that it is told as Nebuchadnezzar's own story. It begins with the king's address to all his realm and then employs the first person in referring to Nebuchadnezzar throughout most of the chapter. It is probable that Nebuchadnezzar himself wrote it, following his shattering experience of insanity. Daniel may have helped him, for there are touches in the chapter that suggest his influence. The fact that Nebuchadnezzar wanted to write such an account is most significant in respect to the total effect this experience had on his life.

A. The Remarkable Introduction (Dan. 4:1-3)

In the first three verses, Nebuchadnezzar gave a significant introduction to the story he was about to relate. He began formally, "Nebuchadnezzar the king, unto all people, nations, and languages," thus addressing the account to everyone in his realm. In much the same way that he previously wanted everyone to know about the fiery furnace event, he now wanted all to know about the time of his insanity. Everyone in the empire would have known, of course, that he had been away from his throne for the seven years involved; so now he used this way to tell them the reason. At the same time, certainly, he wanted to give witness once more to the uniqueness of the God of heaven among all gods including the Babylonian.

In verses 2 and 3, Nebuchadnezzar ascribed remarkable honor to God, saying that He is the "high God," that "his signs" are great and "his wonders" mighty, and that His kingdom is "everlasting," in contrast to any earthly rule. With these words he set the tone for the story to follow, so that the reader could see what the story revealed about this great God of heaven.

B. The Babylonian Wise Men Are Again Frustrated (Dan. 4:4-8)

Having finished the introduction, Nebuchadnezzar took up the narration of the dream. He first told of having the dream and of calling his wise men to interpret it. Daniel, who was still head of the group, did not come at first. He appeared when the others showed themselves inadequate for meeting the king's demand.

The king started the story by speaking of himself as at rest in his house and flourishing in his palace at the time he had the dream.

In other words, everything was going fine for him. But then he had the fearful dream, so that his thoughts distressed him. As a result, he summoned his wise men, according to custom. When they had assembled, he told them the dream, but they did not reveal its interpretation. The fact that they did not calls for notice, because they certainly had books and formulas for doing so, as we noted regarding the first dream. They could have interpreted it, then, in their naturalistic manner, if they had wanted to; this means they did not choose to do so. Probably the reason was that its symbolic significance, even according to their formulas, was too tragic for the king for them to want to convey such information to him.

Finally, Daniel appeared, and then Nebuchadnezzar was relieved. Just why Daniel did not come at first is not indicated. Perhaps God had told him not to arrive at the same time as the others, so that they could again be shown in their inadequacy. This would make Daniel's true interpretation stand out the more forcibly in the king's mind. Even though he came late, Daniel was gladly received by the king, and the king readily repeated the dream for him.

C. The Content of the Dream (Dan. 4:9-18)

Nebuchadnezzar began his narration of the dream with an address to Daniel. He called him by his Babylonian name, Belteshazzar, and indicated that he was still the "master of the magicians" ("magicians" certainly meaning here all wise men), the position Nebuchadnezzar had given him more than thirty years before. Daniel apparently had kept it all these years. He further indicated that "the spirit of the holy god" was in Daniel, a note which is repeated in verses 8 and 18. By this, Nebuchadnezzar may merely have been referring to gods in a general manner, or he may have been thinking of the "spirit of the holy God" in whom Daniel particularly trusted. Because of the context, it seems preferable to take it in the latter sense, for Nebuchadnezzar had come to appreciate this man and his unique contact with His own God, the God of heaven.

The outline of the dream Nebuchadnezzar set forth is as follows. He said he saw a giant tree that could be viewed "to the end of all the earth." Its leaves and fruit were attractive, and it provided shade, and shelter for both animals and birds. Then he saw a heavenly messenger, called a "watcher and an holy one," come down from heaven and call for the tree to be cut down and destroyed, except for its stump. The stump was to remain and be bound with iron and brass; it would stand in the field, with dew falling on it and with beasts of the earth moving about it. Then the heavenly visitor spoke particularly of the stump in a personalized manner to show its symbolism to be of a human being (Nebuchadnezzar himself, as Daniel would later reveal). He said that his heart would be changed from a man's heart to that of a beast; this would continue while "seven times" passed over it. Finally, at the close of the dream, the visitor said the dream's purpose was to show men that the most High rules in the kingdom of men," and that He is in charge of deciding who will rule and who will not. Having finished relating the dream, Nebuchadnezzar exhorted Daniel to give its interpretation.

D. Interpretation of the Dream (Dan. 4:19-27)

Nebuchadnezzar then told of Daniel's reaction to the dream and his interpretation of it. At first, he said, Daniel was silent, which caused Nebuchadnezzar a little concern. Then Daniel began his response by first stating, ominously, that he wished the dream might be for Nebuchadnezzar's enemies rather than himself.

1. The interpretation proper

In his interpretation of the dream, Daniel first made clear that the great tree represented Nebuchadnezzar (vv. 20-22). Nebuchadnezzar, like the tree, had grown great in the earth, with people all over his empire depending on him for sustenance. Then Daniel stated — as perhaps the king had feared — that the cutting down of the tree represented a time of trouble for the king. He would become insane and be driven from among men to live with the animals of the field; this condition would continue until the "seven times" mentioned by the heavenly messenger had elapsed. By that time, the king would know that the most High did rule and give kingdoms to whom He would. A word of hope was included for the king as Daniel added that the continuance of the stump in the field meant that Nebuchadnezzar would continue to live during these seven times, and that he would then rule again. He closed with an admonition to the king to break off with his sins and be merciful to the poor.

2. Some matters to notice in the interpretation

A few matters in this interpretation call for special notice. For one thing, Daniel's hesitation, in remaining silent for a moment before giving the interpretation, showed the king that Daniel had his interest at heart. Daniel wanted the king to know that he would not enjoy relating the interpretation of this dream to him; he said as much when he wished its meaning was in reference to Nebuchadnezzar's enemies rather than Nebuchadnezzar himself.

Then it should be observed that Daniel once more demonstrated true courage in relating such an interpretation to the king, when it meant serious trouble for the monarch. The wise men had hesitated, apparently not daring to speak in such a manner. Daniel, however, did give the narration, clearly and without any omission. He closed his interpretation by giving the king advice: The king should cease in his sin and show mercy to the poor. If he did so, God might show mercy to him and reduce the degree of discipline to be meted out.

Some notice should also be given to the phrase "seven times." The word for "times" was used in three other places in Daniel (2:8; 3:5, 15), but these do not help to know its meaning here for the contexts differ from this instance. In Daniel 7:25, however, it is used in a parallel sense in the phrase "a time and times and the dividing of time." The meaning of the word in this phrase is definitely "year," as will be shown when treating the passage. This meaning also fits for this dream of Nebuchadnezzar. The word cannot be taken to mean a shorter period of time, such as days or even months, for neither would be long enough to be meaningful. A period of seven years, however, fits well with the idea behind the phrase: namely, the full cycle of seasons, with all their changes in types of weather, were made to *pass over* the king seven different times.

Putting together the purpose of the insanity depicted, as indicated in verses 17 and 25, with Daniel's admonition in verse 27, the total reason for the insanity appears as follows: Nebuchadnezzar was seen by God as unusually proud, since he thought of himself as the master of his kingdom, and in this pride he had also become unresponsive to the needs of poor people by not showing proper consideration and mercy toward them. He needed to be humbled and made to realize that the God of heaven was in final charge over all earth's kingdoms, including his own, and he should also show fruit of this humility by being more considerate of the poor.

E. Nebuchadnezzar's Insanity (Dan. 4:28-35)

Nebuchadnezzar's account now told of the fulfillment of the dream's predictions. Nebuchadnezzar did experience the seven years of insanity, but this condition did not come on him immediately. God first gave him twelve months in which to profit from Daniel's advice to humble himself, if he would.

1. The beginning of the insanity (Dan. 4:28-32)

The narration first sets the stage for the fulfillment of the prediction. When the insanity came upon Nebuchadnezzar, twelve months had elapsed following the dream. At that time he was walking *upon* his palace. The palace probably had a flat roof, like that of David's palace (2 Sam. 11:2), and from it the king could see much of splendid Babylon and its fine structures, which he had built. Proud of what he saw, the king voiced the rhetorical question, "Is not this great Babylon that I have built" as a royal city, "by the might of my power and for the honour of my majesty?" (v. 30).

Even as he spoke these words, thus showing that he had indeed not changed during the twelve months given him, a voice from heaven pierced his consciousness. It said that now his kingdom would be taken from him, and he would be driven from among men for seven years, even as the dream had symbolized (vv. 31, 32).

2. The insanity experienced (Dan. 4:33-35)

Nebuchadnezzar said that it was in "the same hour" that his insanity began. This probably means that it came while he was still on the roof, where he had just looked out over his great city. It would have been there, then, that servants soon found him in his deranged condition. A report of the situation would have been communicated quickly to appropriate people, a hurried consultation held, a decision of procedure made, and then carried out. The decision was to take the king out to live among the animals, even as the dream had predicted.

The type of mental illness Nebuchadnezzar suffered is known to medical science and is called "lycanthropy." The victim sees himself as a particular animal and wants to live like that animal. In the most common form the person imagines himself to be a wolf. Nebuchadnezzar clearly saw himself as an ox. The disease, whatever form of animal is involved, is curable and is known to allow the victim sufficient consciousness of self and God to make intelligent prayer possible. Nebuchadnezzar described himself as being put out to live with the oxen of the field, being wet with the dew of heaven, having his hair grow like eagles' feathers and his nails like birds' claws (v. 33).

One need not conclude that Nebuchadnezzar was turned loose to wander wherever he wanted without supervision. It is far more likely that he was placed in some royal forest or on some farm where he could be watched, controlled, and protected from harm. After all, he was still the king, though temporarily incapacitated, and the position called for the finest care that could be given under the circumstances. This special care, in fact, is probably what is signified in the dream by the "band of iron and brass" (v. 15) mentioned by the heavenly messenger. The indication was that the stump (symbolizing Nebuchadnezzar) would be bound, signifying some form of protection that would serve toward the restoration of the king after the completion of the designated seven years. This protection was probably in the form of care by guards, who could only be expected to watch over him in those days of mental helplessness.

Finally, at the end of the set time, Nebuchadnezzar was given enough rationality to raise his eyes to heaven and voice a prayer of humility. He then "praised and honored him that liveth for ever" and voiced his recognition that God has a kingdom that does not end, in His presence all people are really nothing, and on Him all are fully dependent. In other words, Nebuchadnezzar was brought to the place of genuine humility before the God of heaven, even as the dream had indicated would happen. This was the reason for the whole episode. God thus accomplished the purpose that He had planned from the first.

F. Restored to Rule (Dan. 4:36, 37)

Nebuchadnezzar closed his account by stating that he was restored to his place of ruling and, as a result, he was ready to give praise to the God of heaven.

1. *The restoration to rule (Dan. 4:36)*

When Nebuchadnezzar came to this place of acknowledging the supremacy of the God of heaven, then God was ready to restore him to office. His reason returned and with it the glory and honor that he had enjoyed before. His "counsellors and lords" came to him, removed him from the open area where he had spent these years, and established him in his kingdom rule once more. Nebuchadnezzar stated that "excellent majesty was added" to him at the time. The thought no doubt is that he was given even higher honor than before in his kingdom. From the human point of view, this may have been because when the people had to be without his service for this time, they came to recognize how capable a king he had been, and therefore they honored him yet higher on his return. From God's point of view, the purpose would have been to show Nebuchadnezzar that God gives extra honor to those who properly honor Him.

The events that led to this restoration can be imagined in the following manner. The guards watching Nebuchadnezzar would have been quick to recognize a change in his manner when his reason began to return. A report would have been sent immediately to their superiors. Then, when full sanity had been restored, which was probably very soon after, these superiors would have come themselves to see. When convinced that the king was truly well, they would have been quick to restore him to his place of rule. Seven years is a long time for a kingdom to remain without an active head, and kingdom conditons as then existent must have been crying out for this restoration.

The question has often been raised as to how a kingdom like Babylonia would have been willing or able to continue seven years, waiting for Nebuchadnezzar's return. Would the leaders not have sought a permanent replacement long before such a period had elapsed? And could a kingdom, in fact, survive with so long an absence of its head ruler? The answer is best found in three thoughts. The main one is that God simply superintended in the situation so that the people did wait and the kingdom did survive. The divine plan called for Nebuchadnezzar not only to experience the insanity but also to be restored. The means God likely used to bring this about constitute the other two thoughts. One is that Nebuchadnezzar had built a strong organization in his government. As noted in chapter 2, this was mainly why God designated him as the head of gold in his first dream. Able personnel in the various departments could carry on for a substantial time without a head man at the helm. The other thought is that Daniel knew from the start how long the insanity would last and that Nebuchadnezzar would indeed be cured. The dream had indicated this. Because of his high position and influence, Daniel could have, and no doubt did, communicate this information to other key people urging them to make arrangements as best they could until the seven years were finished. Since Daniel enjoyed the finest reputation for honesty and reliability, his words would have carried weight. There may have been some restructuring done to take care of top decision-making, in which, indeed, Daniel himself may have had a part. But such restructuring, with able men available to do the work, could well have been used by God to maintain the kingdom, even as the record indicates.

2. *Nebuchadnezzar's praise of God (Dan. 4:37)*

Nebuchadnezzar's closing words are most significant. They give the reason for his writing the whole account. Having been restored to his throne, he was ready to give due praise to "the King of heaven," recognizing that "those that walk in pride he is able to abase." Nebuchadnezzar had experienced this firsthand, and he had learned his lesson. He was ready to see his place of dependence on this great God and give due honor to His name. The result was that he wrote the account of this chapter and had it published for all his people to read. The effect of such an action could only have been revolutionary. Some people may have thought that the king was still a little insane, but others would have been influenced for good. Surely the God of Daniel came to be respected in a new way throughout the kingdom.

An interesting question concerns whether or not Nebuchadnezzar himself came to exercise personal faith in the God of heaven. The fact that he did pen this record carries significance that he may have. In the record, he expressed some remarkable thoughts regarding Daniel's God. In essence, these thoughts are that this God is supreme in power, having full dominion over all men, is fully equitable in all His works including matters of discipline, and that as a result he, Nebuchadnezzar, was himself giving praise to Him. Because no element of recognizing God's mercy is included, some expositors believe the king fell short of true conversion, and this may certainly be true. On the other hand, what the king does say is most remarkable, when he had previously been a pagan. When all matters are taken together, it seems more probable that he did exercise personal faith than that he did not.

For Further Study

1. Describe the dream which Nebuchadnezzar had in this second instance.
2. Why did the wise men not interpret this dream?
3. What evidence exists that Daniel admired Nebuchadnezzar as a king?
4. Why do you believe God warned Nebuchadnezzar ahead of time through this dream that he would become insane?
5. Describe the mental disease that came on Nebuchadnezzar.
6. What was the purpose of God's sending this punishment on Nebuchadnezzar? Was it achieved?

Chapter 5

Miraculous Writing Interpreted

Chapter 5 again presents the words of Daniel himself. He did not quote the words of another, as in the previous chapter, but told the events as he remembered them. The story concerns the dramatic occasion when Belshazzar, a new king of Babylonia, witnessed supernatural writing on his palace wall and had to look to Daniel for its interpretation.

The story occurred many years after the time of Nebuchadnezzar's second dream. Belshazzar was now ruling, and several kings had intervened since Nebuchadnezzar. In fact, Belshazzar himself was not the only king of the land at the time, but served as coregent with his father, Nabonidus (556-539 B.C.). Nabonidus was of a different ruling family from that of Nebuchadnezzar, having assassinated his predecessor, Labashi-marduk, with the help of a group of dissatisfied courtiers. Nabonidus, however spent long periods of time away from his throne, and for this reason he installed his eldest son, Belshazzar, as coruler with himself in 553 B.C. Both then ruled until 539 B.C., when Cyrus captured Babylon for Medo-Persia. This story occurred on the same date as that capture, for Belshazzar was killed that very night (Dan. 5:30). This means that approximately thirty-two years had elapsed since Nebuchadnezzar's second dream, and Daniel was now about eighty-one years old.

Nabonidus was not in Babylon at the time the story occurred, which is the reason he is not mentioned in it. His existence as coruler, however, is significantly implied in one of the rewards that Belshazzar bestowed on Daniel for interpreting the miraculous writing. He made him "third ruler" in the kingdom rather than second (Dan. 5:29; cf. v. 16). He could not make him second because he was himself second, since his father was first.

In passing, it may be observed that, for many years, liberal writers declared that Belshazzar was unhistorical and the book of Daniel was in error in speaking of him as Babylonia's last king. It was known that Nabonidus held this position, and the existence of Belshazzar was unknown from ancient records then in hand. There is now ample evidence, however, that Belshazzar, as Nabonidus' eldest son, was made coregent with his father and did serve as king while his father was away from home. The Bible has again been proven accurate and the liberal critics wrong.

A. An Impious Feast (Dan. 5:1-4)

The story begins with the account of a great feast put on by Belshazzar. It was at this feast that the miraculous writing appeared.

1. *The general setting (Dan. 5:1)*

The setting of the feast is first presented. That the king should have made such a feast, to which he invited "a thousand of his lords," seems unusual in view of the situation. The city was in imminent danger of falling to the Medo-Persians, for, as noted, it was in the same night as this feast that the city fell. One would think that Belshazzar would have been occupied with defense activities rather than a feast. It may be, however, that the feast itself was intended as a type of defense activity, that is, a way in which to build morale among the leaders. The city had been under siege for some time,[1] and it could be that everything physically possible for defense had already been done. Belshazzar, then, may have seen morale building as his most important task. The feast could show his leaders that he as king was not worried at all; he could even enjoy a banquet while the enemy waited outside Babylon's impregnable walls.

Whatever Belshazzar's intentions, however, it is certain that everyone who attended the feast was extremely conscious of the imminent danger. They could not really forget the army that was encamped outside the walls. The outwardly carefree atmosphere at the feast, then, must have been fragile and altogether artificial. The occasion, therefore, provided an excellent setting for the miraculous writing that God would soon make to appear.

The phrase of verse 1, that the king "drank wine before the thousand," deserves notice. Oriental custom called for the king to sit at a separate table at such feasts; there he could give guidance for attitude,

---

[1] Several records of this occasion exist; see p. 76.

atmosphere, and tempo. The notice here that Belshazzar drank wine before the others is to say that he was setting the atmosphere as one of carefree hilarity. All present, then, should not only feel free to follow his lead but make it a point to do so.

In keeping with this indication, the archeologist Koldeway,[2] who excavated Babylon, found what is likely the very room in which this banquet took place; the room suits all that is said about it in this story. I have personally stood in this room. It measures 165 feet long by 55 feet wide, and has plastered walls (see Dan. 5:5). Most of the plaster is now gone, but the remains of the walls still stand several feet high. Especially important is the niche at the middle of one of the longer walls, directly opposite the door of entrance into the room. It is here that the king would have sat, no doubt on a slightly raised platform, so that he could be seen by all present.

2. The feast (Dan. 5:2-4)

The feast was very large, having one thousand in attendance. This was not really unusual in ancient time, however. Persian rulers later sometimes fed as many as fifteen thousand at one time (cf. Esther 1:4). The reference in verse 2 that Belshazzar was tasting the wine is indicative of two things. One is that the eating part of the feast had been completed at this point and the drinking time had arrived; such a drinking time normally followed eating. The other is that this tasting influenced him in making the decision to bring in the sacred vessels of Jerusalem. This was an unusual order. Seized sacred vessels of a foreign country were not normally used in this way. Nebuchadnezzar, who had taken them years before (Dan. 1:2; cf. 2 Kings 24:13; 25:13-17), had put them in "the house of his god," and apparently left them there in accordance with accepted proprieties. Not so Belshazzar, however. The tasting of the wine apparently dulled his sense of propriety and judgment.

The context implies that at least two reasons motivated him in this demand, improper as it was. First, such valuable drinking containers obviously would add luster to the grand occasion. The text specifically says that he ordered the gold and silver vessels. Other vessels that had been taken may have been made of lesser metals, but he wanted the finest. These would have been the ones made principally by Solomon (see 1 Kings 7:47-51; 10:21). Second, Belshazzar clearly wanted to bring dishonor on the God of Judah,

---

[2]Koldewey, *Das wieder erstehende Babylon,* quoted by James Montgomery, *Commentary on the Book of Daniel,* p. 253.

whose vessels they were. This is made evident by the significant words of verses 3 and 4, by Daniel's words to Belshazzar that the king had "lifted up [himself] against the Lord of heaven" in doing this (Dan. 5:23), and also by God's use of this occasion to warn and punish the king, showing that Belshazzar had truly been acting in a way to deserve such punishment. It would appear that Belshazzar, knowing of Nebuchadnezzar's earlier humiliation before the God of Judah (Dan. 5:22), had reacted in a resolve not to be intimidated himself and even to demonstrate open defiance. It could be that in God's providence a recent reminder of Nebuchadnezzar's experience had come his way, and this prompted his provocative order.

Verse 2 (cf. vv. 11, 13, 18, 22) refers to Nebuchadnezzar as Belshazzar's father. Since Nebuchadnezzar was not the immediate father of Belshazzar (Nabonidus was his father, and he was even of a different family), this statement has been challenged for its accuracy. However, Belshazzar may well have been the grandson of Nebuchadnezzar through his mother, and the word used can mean grandfather as well as father. If this is correct, Belshazzar's mother would probably have been Nitocris, wife of Nabonidus and daughter of the great Nebuchadnezzar.[3] If this explanation should possibly prove incorrect, it is a known fact that simply a successor on a throne could be called a son of his predecessor. The Assyrian emperor, Shalmaneser III, on his famous Black Obelisk, spoke of Jehu, the Israelite king, as "son of Omri," though they were completely unrelated (see 2 Kings 9, 10).[4]

Verses 2 and 3 both speak of "wives and concubines"[5] drinking, as well as the lords. Apparently, female companions now joined the festivities, and no doubt the occasion soon degenerated to a drunken revelry. Alcohol has caused untold sin and wickedness through the ages. But verse 4 tells of the greatest sin at the feast. The drunken throng, led by the defiant king, drank from the vessels of the true God and at the same time "praised the gods of gold, and of silver, of brass, of iron, of wood, and of stone" (v. 4). That is to say, these sacred cups were employed — deliberately in defiance of the God

[3]For discussion, see R. P. Dougherty, *Nabonidus and Belshazzar.*

[4]For the text, see J. B. Pritchard, ed., *Ancient Near Eastern Texts,* p. 281. R. D. Wilson lists seven ways in which the term "father" was used in Nebuchadnezzar's time and twelve ways in which "son" was used (*Studies in Daniel,* pp. 117, 118).

[5]Concubines were considered to be wives, but of a secondary status.

of Judah — to give praise to Babylonia's false gods. This was the height of insolence in the sight of God, and Belshazzar would soon hear from Him as a result.

B. The Miraculous Writing (Dan. 5:5-9)

As the drunken revelry progressed, suddenly fingers, as of a human hand, appeared, writing on a well-lighted portion of the wall. Everyone, including the king, was immediately struck with terror. The king quickly called for the wise men to come, but they were unable to read the writing, which set the scene most propitiously for the entrance of Daniel.

1. *The miracle (Dan. 5:5)*

God suddenly brought the hilarity of the occasion to a halt, as He made fingers appear, writing on the palace wall. How little God had to do to bring a complete change of atmosphere! One may imagine that goblets of wine, being raised to waiting lips, stopped in midair and conversations ceased with words partially pronounced and never finished. All eyes turned to the one place on the wall, which, significantly, was well-lighted by a nearby lamp (v. 5). There they saw the fingers moving and writing on the wall. Finally the fingers disappeared, but the writing remained for all to see and ponder. All eyes were turned toward the king. What would be his attitude now?

Before noting Belshazzar's own attitude, it is important to consider this handwriting as a method by which to speak to this pagan king and his officers. God regularly fits methods to needs, and He did here. Dreams had been suitable to employ with Nebuchadnezzar, for he alone was involved. In the present case, however, others beside the king had to be impressed as well. Also there was a need now for a continuing sign, one that would remain for some hours and so be the more impressive. This would fix its reality more firmly in mind, and, besides, no one could later say that someone only thought he saw something miraculous for a fleeting moment. The writing, further, provided an objective sign that the king could not change or manipulate to his advantage in any way. It also required an interpreter, just as Nebuchadnezzar's dreams did, necessitating the call for Daniel.

2. *The king's fear (Dan. 5:6)*

As the people turned toward the king, they saw a man filled with terror. From a drunken egotist who defied the God of heaven, he had become a man cringing in fright, "so that the joints of his loins were loosed, and his knees smote one against another." Belshazzar realized that he was seeing a miracle, and he no doubt recognized also that this could only be from the God of Judah, whom he had just been defying. Certainly the memory of the awful punishment experienced by Nebuchadnezzar flashed through his mind. He must also have thought of the Medo-Persian hosts just outside Babylon's walls. He could only conclude that catastrophe of some kind was surely at hand. This is a most significant illustration of how easily God can change the manner of man's thinking and attitude.

3. The wise men summoned (Dan. 5:7-9)

Immediately Belshazzar reacted as Nebuchadnezzar had before him; he called for his wise men to tell him what the writing meant. When they arrived, Belshazzar further showed his emotional disturbance by promising unusual rewards to whoever could read and interpret the writing. He would be given a purple robe (the word translated in the King James Version as "scarlet" is better rendered "purple"), which was worn only by royalty, and a gold chain which was customarily worn only by ranking officials; he also would be made a "third ruler" in the kingdom. The word for "third ruler" may signify actually a "triumvir," meaning a third member of a coequal group of three rulers.

In spite of the attractive incentives, the assembled group could not do as the king desired; they could neither read nor interpret the writing. Why they could not at least read it is not easily determined, for it was in Aramaic, and Aramaic was well known in Babylon by this time. Perhaps God intentionally had the letters shaped in an unusual manner or arrangement, so that even Daniel could not have read them without special insight granted by God. It should be realized, also, that this type of problem would have been unique to these wise men. They were accustomed to interpreting dreams, for which their books gave them formulas of interpretation, but miraculous writing on a wall was completely new and different. Perhaps this very uniqueness made them hesitate to even try to give either a reading or an interpretation; such writing was too clearly out of their domain, too supernatural for them to want to have anything to do with it. But when they indicated that they could not do what the king wanted, the king and his lords really became disturbed. If these men could not give the meaning, then where could they turn for help?

C. Daniel Summoned (Dan. 5:10-16)

These developments proved highly advantageous for Daniel's arrival. He was the one man in Belshazzar's kingdom who could both read and interpret the writing.

God arranged for Daniel's entrance through another person who now came into the room. She is called simply "the queen," and she apparently had not been present earlier; but now she did arrive, perhaps as a result of hearing the commotion going on. She was probably the queen mother, rather than the wife of Belshazzar. His wife was almost certainly already present (v. 2); besides this person demonstrated unusual knowledge of former days, when Nebuchadnezzar had lived. This queen mother was very likely Nitocris, mentioned earlier, who was the daughter of Nebuchadnezzar and therefore would have had this historical familiarity. She now told her son, Belshazzar, about Daniel and explained that Nebuchadnezzar — whom she significantly referred to as Belshazzar's father, even three times in one verse[6] (v. 11) — had found him capable of giving such interpretations as Belshazzar now needed. Because she referred to Daniel at first by the introductory phrase, "There is a man," it is likely that Daniel no longer held his high position as chief of the wise men. This is understandable in view of Daniel's age and also because several kings had ruled since Nebuchadnezzar. He still held some position, however, according to Daniel 8:27 (cf. 8:1), and must not have lived far from the palace in holding that position, for he was able to be present very quickly after being summoned.

Belshazzar did immediately call for him. The queen mother had extolled him highly, and Belshazzar was quite ready to listen to anyone who might give help in the frightening situation. The fact that the queen mother had praised Daniel in such laudatory terms is in keeping with the deep impression Daniel had made on Nebuchadnezzar. It suggests, in fact, that what was presented in the former chapter as a possibility for the former king was true; namely, that he had given true allegiance to Daniel's God and, further, that this had even been shared by this daughter.

Belshazzar's first question to Daniel on his arrival shows that he himself may not have been as ignorant of this man as the queen mother implied in her statement. He asked if he was indeed the

[6]See explanation under v. 2. She evidently believed that her counsel to Belshazzar would be more persuasive if he was impressed with this father-son relationship to the one who had previously so honored Daniel.

Daniel who had been brought captive from Judah by Nebuchadnezzar. In other words, he knew of Daniel, but apparently had not met him face to face before. He may not have wanted to meet him before, in light of his attitude as shown in this feast. Daniel had been the one who had predicted Nebuchadnezzar's insanity, and Belshazzar wanted to avoid anything like this for himself. Now, however, he was in a position where he had no choice, and he wanted to be sure that this aged person was really the same one who had given interpretation for his "father." The fact, of course, that Daniel represented the very God whom he, Belshazzar, had just been defying was very much in back of this question of identification. Was Daniel really the one taken captive at the time these vessels of Judah had been brought to Babylon?

Thinking in this manner regarding the man standing before him, Belshazzar certainly feared what he might have to say. It could only be very unpleasant, but Belshazzar still had to know what this writing — which was surely sent by this same God Daniel represented — meant. Thus, he had to listen, whether the information would be distressing or not. God has His own way of putting even kings in situations where they have no alternative but to do as He desires. Accordingly, Belshazzar proceeded to tell Daniel of the failure of his wise men and that he had learned that Daniel could interpret such matters as this writing. He even promised Daniel the same three attractive honors that he had promised the wise men if he could now do what they had failed to do.

D. The Interpretation (Dan. 5:17-28)

Daniel responded by first refusing the king's honors — certainly surprising the king in this, for it was so abnormal. The reason no doubt was that Daniel did not want to be under any obligation to speak only what the king wanted to hear. Then he stirred the king's memory by recalling for him the experience of Nebuchadnezzar, when he was humbled through insanity by the God of heaven. Only then did he give the interpretation itself.

1. *Introductory matters (Dan. 5:17-21)*

As Daniel began to speak, it was a highly significant moment for him. He had known of this king (who was much younger than himself, of course) and had no doubt wished many times to witness to him as he had to Nebuchadnezzar; now he had the opportunity,

arranged clearly by God. After first refusing the king's honors, he
made a major point of recalling for the king the experience of Nebuchadnezzar. He reminded Belshazzar in some detail how the former
ruler, great and powerful as he was, had been made to dwell in the
fields and live like the animals. He told him that the purpose had
been to humble Nebuchadnezzar and make him know that "God
ruled in the kingdom of men." This sort of message, of course, Belshazzar did not want to hear. He had just been defying the God of
whom Daniel spoke, and he was in no frame of mind to want to be
reminded of this past history. Daniel, however, knew that this
reminder was just what the king needed to hear, and he courageously
gave it. The important matter was not what the king wanted, but
what God wanted. Daniel again set an excellent example of courage
and obedience.

2. Belshazzar's own pride (Dan. 5:22, 23)

Then Daniel came to the point of this historical recital. Belshazzar
was much like Nebuchadnezzar for he was proud also. The phrase
"though you knew all this" is especially noteworthy. Daniel meant
to say that Belshazzar, in his pride — as shown especially in his
recent defiance at the feast — knew of this past history but still had
not learned the lesson of humility himself. Then Daniel reminded
the king of that recent defiance, even mentioning specifically the
sacred vessels of "the Lord of heaven" being used for drinking while
the false gods of Babylon were worshipped. Daniel's intention, of
course, was to prepare the king for the important interpretation of
the writing that he would soon give. Significantly, the king did not
blurt out any rebuke of Daniel, in spite of the directness of Daniel's
words. The reason can only be that he was fearful because of the
miraculous writing. Had Daniel spoken in this manner before the
writing appeared, while the feast was in progress, Belshazzar would
have raged with fury and, no doubt, ordered Daniel's death. God
can change the hardest hearts in a very short time.

3. The interpretation given (Dan. 5:24-28)

The implication is clear that the writing was still visible on the
wall as Daniel came to the point of reading and interpreting it. Surely
several hours of the evening had elapsed since it first appeared, for
the wise men had come, then the queen mother made her presentation, and finally Daniel was summoned and arrived. All this time the
writing had remained to make its strong impression on all assem-

bled. Very likely, no one present at its appearance had left, either; the matter was too important.

According to the king's desire, Daniel first read the writing and then explained it. The reading did not take long, for there were only four words: "Mene, Mene, Tekel, Upharsin." The very brevity made the writing the more impressionable and also easier to retain in one's memory.

"Mene," as Daniel explained, means "numbered," or, more fully in this context: God had numbered the days of Belshazzar's kingdom and, as a result, now considered them as having come to an end. This word was used twice, evidently for emphasis. "Tekel" means "weighed"; or, more fully: God had weighed Belshazzar's conduct as king and found it lacking. "Upharsin" ("peres," v. 28, where it is used without the conjunction "u" and the plural ending "in") means "divided" or "broken into pieces"; or again more fully in context: Belshazzar's kingdom was to be broken in pieces and given to the Medes and Persians, who were even then at the gate of the city.

Daniel thus pronounced the doom that Belshazzar feared. The God whom he had been defying was about to bring punishment on him, even as He had on Nebuchadnezzar years before, only now in a more severe manner. The enemy forces outside Babylon's walls would be victorious. Babylon was about to fall. Belshazzar's days as king were at an end. Daniel did not indicate how long it would be before this would happen — indeed, he may not have known — but Belshazzar found out before that night was over.

Man likes to think of himself as self-sufficient, so that he can do as he pleases without having to look to God for help or fear Him for retribution. Belshazzar wanted to think this way, but he found that he could not. God knew about him and would now indeed bring the retribution. God knows about the sin of all men, and His requirement is that all sin be paid for, one way or another. How important it is that men look to God and seek the way of deliverance that He has provided.

E. The Result (Dan. 5:29-31)

The last three verses indicate the results of these surprising developments.

The first was that Belshazzar, instead of being angry with Daniel for his direct words, still wanted to honor him with the promised gifts. And Daniel did accept, now that the uninfluenced message had been given. No longer could one say that he had been under pressure to conform the interpretation to what the king might find pleasant — especially in view of the nature of the message he had presented. He was given the royal-colored robe, the gold chain, and made "third ruler" or "triumvir" in the kingdom. The objection has been raised that so much could not have been given that evening. There would not have been great difficulty, however. Both the robe and chain could have been brought quickly, and the announcement of the honored position could have been meaningfully given before all the officials there present, with the public announcement intended as soon as conditions would permit. The observation has been made that, actually, the honors were of little significance, since Belshazzar was killed that very night. It turned out this way, true enough, but at the moment no one there — including Daniel, very likely — knew just how long the time would be. The honors were genuine enough when given.

The second result was that Belshazzar was indeed killed that very night. The Medo-Persian host did invade the city and Belshazzar was a principal casualty (v. 30). The story of the fall of Babylon has been found in four separate sources. They are the historical accounts of Herodotus and Xenophon (of the fifth and fourth centuries B.C. respectively) and the cuneiform records of both Nabonidus and Cyrus of this very occasion. Both Herodotus and Xenophon tell of the Euphrates River, which flowed under the wall of Babylon and through the city, as being diverted so that the riverbed could be used to enter. Neither of the original cuneiform records tells of this aspect of the city's capture, but they do indicate that the fall of the city was remarkably free from bloodshed. Xenophon tells of drunken feasting as being in progress in the city at its fall. Both his and Nabonidus' records indicate that the commander of the Medo-Persian force at the time was not Cyrus himself (who was temporarily absent for some reason) but a general named Ugbaru. Nabonidus' record also makes clear that the king within Babylon, when the capture was effected, was not Nabonidus but Belshazzar. Nabonidus had fled earlier and was seized only later after Babylon had been taken. All these facts fit well with the account of Daniel.

The third result was that the Medo-Persians took over the rule of the city and empire, with Darius the Mede being installed as king. He was already sixty-two years old (v. 31). Actually Cyrus was the first king of the Medo-Persians, and this Darius was installed by him as king over the Babylon portion of the larger territory he controlled.

For Further Study

1. Read articles in a Bible dictionary or encyclopedia on: (a) Belshazzar, (b) Nabonidus, (c) Cyrus.

2. For what reason may Belshazzar have made his feast when the city of Babylon was under siege by the Medo-Persians?

3. What was Belshazzar's worst sin committed at this feast?

4. Describe the change that came at the feast when the fingers appeared writing on the wall.

5. How would you characterize the words of the queen mother concerning Daniel?

6. Why did Daniel first tell Belshazzar about Nebuchadnezzar?

7. Summarize the message that was written on the wall.

8. Characterize Belshazzar's thinking when told this message.

Chapter 6

Daniel and the Lions' Den

In this chapter, the interest turns to one of the best-known stories of the Bible, the occasion of Daniel in the den of lions. The jealousy of political subordinates brought about this terrible sentence for Daniel. But God effected a miraculous deliverance for him, even as He had for the three friends earlier in the fiery furnace.

Politically, the situation was quite different from that of the prior chapters. Then Babylon had been the country in control; now it was Medo-Persia. The exact length of time that had passed since the fall of Babylon cannot be determined, but at least a few months had elapsed, for the new regime was now established and jealousies had been formed. Probably no less than two years had gone by, meaning that Daniel was about eighty-three.

The identity of the Medo-Persian ruler in the story, Darius the Mede, has long been questioned. No one of this name is known from secular history, and it is well established that Cyrus continued as head ruler over the empire until 529 B.C., nine years after Babylon's fall. Three principal views have been set forth by scholars: that Darius was Cyrus himself, under a different name here in Daniel; that he was Cambyses, the son of Cyrus who later became Cyrus' full successor but here could have served temporarily as ruler only of Babylonia; or that he was one named Gubaru in secular sources, who is known to have been appointed governor over Babylonia by Cyrus immediately after the fall of the city. Of the three, the last is the most probable.[1]

Putting together all information known regarding this Gubaru, whether from secular records or from Daniel's account, the following picture appears. He was born in 601 B.C. of one named Ahasuerus, a Mede, and was appointed by Cyrus as governor or "king" ("king" in a

[1]For discussion, see J. Whitcomb, *Darius the Mede*.

the basis of their own records. But the text states flatly that "they could find none occasion nor fault" regarding him. This was most remarkable. Certainly Daniel, being in the high position he held, would have had a large staff of people working under him, and these would have all been investigated as well. Daniel must not only have been personally honest, but he must have picked assistants who maintained similar standards. Anyone in a parallel position of superintendence can appreciate what this meant in regard to Daniel's executive ability. How good it would be if all Christians, whatever their position, could be found as guiltless if similarly investigated.

2. *A decree signed (Dan. 6:5-9)*

As a result, the conspirators realized they would have to look elsewhere for their cause if they were to bring a charge against Daniel; so they decided on a course of action involving Daniel's faithfulness to his God. That they did so was really a compliment for Daniel. They were sufficiently impressed by his religious faithfulness to believe they could build a plot against him based on it. They now came as a group to the king to urge that he sign a special decree they had written. It read that anyone who made a request "of any god or man for thirty days" except of Darius should "be cast into the den of lions" (v. 7). To impress the king and to gain his signature on the decree, they asserted that all the king's official family had agreed on this edict, which could hardly have been true. At least Daniel had not agreed, and very likely those officers in outlying districts had not either.

The den of lions they had in mind was apparently an underground cavity (perhaps an adapted natural cave) with an opening at the top. Daniel is said to have been drawn up out of it (v. 23), and later the conspirators, when cast in, were eaten by the lions before they came to "the bottom of the den" (v. 24). It may also have had a side entrance through which to let lions in and out, but that may not have been used often. The den must have been large to allow for several lions to move about and also to permit all the conspirators and their families to be cast into it at one time (v. 24). Such a place would have been most foreboding to people. The lions would have been kept nicely hungry, so that they would quickly devour anyone cast within as punishment. Which form of punishment would be more terrifying, the fiery furnace of Shadrach, Meshach, and Abednego, or this den of lions of Daniel, is difficult to say. Both were of the very worst to contemplate.

Darius now displayed his vanity as he felt flattered by this remarkable honor seemingly accorded him, and he foolishly signed the decree. Had he waited to do so, he might have made some inquiry which would have revealed the plot involved, but he did not. He signed, and when he did the decree became permanently binding. An integral part of the plot was based on the fact that any law of the Medes and Persians could not be changed (see vv. 8, 12, 15).

C. Faithfulness and Accusation (Dan. 6:10-15)

1. *Daniel's continued faithfulness in prayer (Dan. 6:10)*

One of Scripture's outstanding examples of courageous obedience is now presented. The information regarding the decree soon reached Daniel, and it may be assumed that he, being knowledgeable and wise, quickly recognized what was behind it. However, he did not change his manner before God. He proceeded with his normal schedule of prayer, coming before God three times daily, just as before. Verse 10 says significantly that, on learning of the matter, Daniel "went into his house; and his window being open in his chamber toward Jerusalem, he kneeled upon his knees three times a day." Daniel might have reacted quite differently and still rationalized that he was acting acceptably in God's sight. He might have reasoned that he would simply cease praying for the thirty days indicated in the decree and then start again; after all, God would understand. Or he might have thought of praying privately, in a closed room, where he would not be seen. He would still be praying, but no one would have any reason to report him to the king.

Daniel did not rationalize in any such manner, however, and there was an important reason. He had been a strong testimony for his God all his life, telling how his God could provide for those who trusted Him. If he should now even appear to stop praying to this God, all his previous testimony would be irreparably hurt. People would think that he had not meant what he had said after all. Therefore, Daniel concluded that the maintenance of his testimony was more important than the continuance of his life. For this reason, he prayed as before, whatever the outcome. What a challenge again he gives to every believer!

Verse 10 indicates that Daniel's "chamber" had windows that opened toward Jerusalem. It was before these that Daniel customarily prayed, where anyone passing could see him, and it was here that he now continued to pray. Solomon had suggested the propriety of facing the Temple in prayer (see 1 Kings 8:33, 35, 38, 44, 48), and David seems to have practiced the idea already in his day (see Ps. 5:7; 28:2). When the people were taken captive, the gesture became even more significant, for it symbolized the direction of their heart's desire. The three times Daniel prayed were probably morning, noon, and night of each day. To have maintained such a schedule, even in normal times, would have required remarkable discipline of life, especially when Daniel had such a high position with all its necessary duties. He now continued the schedule even in the face of danger.

2. *The accusation of the plotters (Dan. 6:11-15)*

The leaders of the plot were on hand to observe what Daniel would do. They no doubt knew his time schedule and made sure they were in a position to watch him when the first time for his prayer arrived following the official announcement of the king. Whether they let Daniel know of their presence or whether they simply located themselves where they could see him without letting him know is not indicated. They did see, and then they went quickly to report to the king. In their resulting accusation, they spoke of Daniel as "of the children of the captivity of Judah," thus again identifying the one charged as a Jew. Since Darius knew Daniel so well, there surely was no need for this descriptive note. That they included it, shows once more a vindictive attitude toward anyone from Judah.

It was at this point that the king realized what had happened; he had been a tool in a vicious plot. Accordingly, he now became "sore displeased with himself" (v. 14). He was "sore displeased" with these men, too, of course. They had flattered him into an unjust action. Consequently, he tried to get out of the trap, laboring "till the going down of the sun to deliver" Daniel. His efforts were of no avail, however, for the Medo-Persian law could not be changed. The accusers had hoped, of course, that his reaction would be to show anger against Daniel for having defied his decree; but Darius knew Daniel too well for this. It was not for nothing that he had thought to elevate Daniel, and his reaction, therefore, was to the detriment of these men, not of Daniel.

When the day came to a close, with all Darius' efforts in Daniel's behalf having proven futile, the accusers returned to him. They reminded him once more that the law of the Medes and Persians could not be changed, which certainly did not help endear them to the king, who had just worked against that fact for several hours.

Their reminder, no doubt, helped to assure their own sentence of death, when later Daniel came to be delivered from the fate they planned for him.

D. Sentence and Deliverance (Dan. 6:16-23)

1. *Daniel's sentence (Dan. 6:16, 17)*

Finally, Darius gave the order for Daniel to be apprehended. He had done all he could to avoid having to issue it, but oriental custom was that the execution of a sentence had to be carried out before the end of the day when the accusation was made. Daniel thus was taken and brought to the lions' den. At the time of this arrest, Daniel was probably made aware for the first time of the result of his continued prayer time. At the moment, it would have been easy to think that God had forgotten him. Years before, the same could have been thought by the three friends when faced with the fiery furnace. Now it was Daniel's turn, and it may be assumed that he, like them, faced the challenge with equal commitment to God.

As Daniel was brought to the place of execution, the king himself was there, and he did the amazing thing of trying to console the one whom he had sentenced. He said to Daniel, "Your God whom you serve continually will deliver you" (v. 16). This remarkable statement from the king and his following actions reveal that Daniel had told him much regarding the true God. Daniel had not let Darius' high position stop him, as he had not in the cases of Nebuchadnezzar and Belshazzar earlier. He had been a faithful witness to all. This remark by Darius, in fact, along with his later actions, makes one wonder if he had possibly come to place his personal trust in this God of Daniel. Certainly he had come to respect Him highly, meaning that Daniel's testimony had borne at least this much fruit. Too often Christians are reluctant to witness to people in high positions, but this should not be.

With this statement by Darius made, the order was carried out. Daniel was given to the hungry lions, and a stone cover was set in place and sealed with the official stamps of both the king and his lords. Such a seal was made of wax or soft clay, imprinted with the officials' stamps. The significance of the double stamp was that the stone could not be moved without the permission of both the king and these lesser officials. The stone may have been at the side entrance rather than the top, since Daniel's rescue from the den the following morning took place presumably before any of the lords were present (v. 24).

2. *God's deliverance of Daniel (Dan. 6:18-23)*

Darius returned to his palace, but only to spend a miserable evening and night. He did not eat, nor were any forms of normal entertainment brought before him. The reason clearly was that he regretted so much what had happened. He did not wish to lose such a valuable officer as Daniel, and he felt guilty for the unwitting part he had played in the matter. When he tried to sleep, he could not do this, his mind, no doubt, unceasingly reviewing the events of the day.

The result was that at the first light of morning he was on his way to the den of lions, perhaps even before others were yet awake in the city. Reaching the place, he called out "with a lamentable voice," to Daniel, whom he no doubt could not see in the darkness of the den below: "O Daniel, servant of the living God, is thy God, whom thou servest continually, able to deliver thee from the lions?" The fact that Darius even thought such a deliverance possible shows how high a respect he had gained for Daniel's God. Certainly this was a remarkable situation: a king, early in the morning, calling down into a den of lions, to which he had sentenced a man, asking if the man's God had somehow been able to save him and hoping that it was true! Has ever another occasion happened like it?

Back from the black depths below came Daniel's response: "My God hath sent his angel and hath shut the lions' mouths, that they have not hurt me." No such indication is given, but it may well be that Daniel had actually slept better in the lions' den than the king had in his royal bedroom. Possibly the king's call had awakened him. God had shut the mouths of the great beasts so that they had not hurt him any more than the fiery furnace had hurt his friends. His indication that God's angel had shut the lions' mouths may indicate that he had enjoyed the presence of this heavenly messenger in the den, in parallel with the experience of his three friends in the furnace.

Daniel's response to the king's query must have given great relief to the worried ruler. He was probably surprised that such a thing had really happened, but very happy that it had. As he realized the full import of Daniel's reply, he would have had even more reason for giving personal allegiance to this great God of Daniel. It would be nice to think that he did, but of this nothing is said definitely. He did give immediate orders that Daniel be lifted out of the confining den; when he was, no harm whatever was found on him, though, no doubt, a careful investigation was made. But no evidence was found that the lions had been able to hurt Daniel any more than the fire had hurt Shadrach, Meshach, and Abed-nego.

E. Two Significant Results (Dan. 6:24-28)

1. *The accusers punished (Dan. 6:24)*

With Daniel spared from death, the king gave an order that his accusers be brought, along with their families, and be consigned to the death they had intended for Daniel. What a complete change this was for the plotters. The night before they thought they had won in their designs against this man. Now they were all apprehended themselves, brought to the same den from which Daniel had been delivered, and given to the lions. Daniel was probably put in through a side door, as noted, but these were cast in from above, for it is said that their bones were broken in pieces by the lions before "ever they came at the bottom of the den" (v. 24). The seal bearing their stamps may still have been on the side door when they were cast in from the top opening. Again, God's principle came true: "Whatsoever a man soweth, that shall he also reap" (Gal. 6:7).

2. *A God-honoring decree (Dan. 6:25-28)*

Darius followed this order by issuing a decree to all his domain, as Nebuchadnezzar had many years before. The central message of the decree was that all people of his realm were to "tremble and fear before the God of Daniel" (v. 26). Darius gave four reasons for this: because this God is the living God; because He is "stedfast for ever" (that is, He endures forever); because His kingdom will "not be destroyed," (meaning that it, too, will remain forever); and because He delivers and rescues, as He had just done in delivering "Daniel from the power of the lions" (vv. 26, 27).

Such a decree from a ruler raised in paganism was most remarkable. The truths stated would have been unusual had the man only believed them himself, apart from making a public declaration of this kind. But he set them forth as an official edict for all to read. Certainly this suggests some change of heart on his part. One may hope that it was genuine and that the decree issued encouraged others to follow his lead.

The last verse (v. 28) indicates that Daniel continued to prosper during Darius' rule. The further statement that this was also during the reign of Cyrus does not mean that Cyrus followed Darius. As has been noted, the two served contemporaneously. Daniel continued to prosper during the rule of both, as they served at the same time. The force of the statement is to say that, whereas Daniel's accusers all died in the lions' den, Daniel, who had remained true to God in spite of their efforts, continued to live and prosper. He probably, in fact, received the advanced position planned for him by Darius, with new appointees made to serve under him. Surely this testifies once more to God's faithfulness to those who are faithful to Him.

For Further Study

1. Read an article in a Bible dictionary or encyclopedia on: Darius the Mede.
2. What would have been Daniel's work as one of the three top presidents?
3. What was so unusual about Daniel holding this high position in the new Medo-Persian government?
4. Where did Daniel's enemies first look for an accusation to use against him?
5. What is taught in this chapter in respect to a proper attitude toward flattery?
6. When did the king first realize that he had been tricked?
7. Why was it important that Daniel continue to pray *before his window* after he had learned of the decree?
8. What evidence does the story show that Daniel had been witnessing to Darius concerning the true God?
9. What parallels can you find between Daniel's experience here and that of his three friends in chapter three?
10. How would you characterize Daris' thinking regarding Daniel's God after this occasion was over?

CHRONOLOGY OF DANIEL'S PROPHECIES

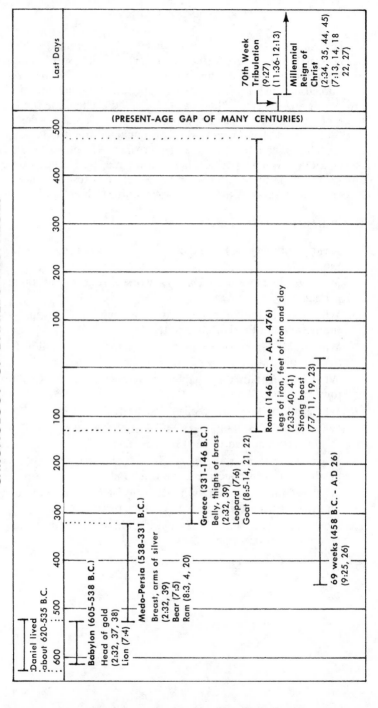

Chapter 7

The First Vision: The Four Empires

This chapter begins the second division of the book. The first six chapters have been mainly historical, with a minimum of prediction; the second division is mainly predictive, with a minimum of history.

These predictions were given through four separate visions, which Daniel saw at four different times within the historical period already covered. The first vision, given in this present chapter, is the most comprehensive, covering the entire course of events involved in all the visions. The others all concern portions of this total sweep of history. The four world empires symbolized in Nebuchadnezzar's first dream constitute the theme; they are the Babylonian, Medo-Persian, Grecian, and Roman Empires. Nebuchadnezzar's dream and this vision of Daniel have numerous parallels.

One of these parallels concerns an extensive gap in time symbolized in respect to the fourth empire (the Roman). This gap falls between the close of that empire of ancient time and a restored form of it still to come. The time-gap, or rather the restoration of the empire which makes for the gap, is necessary to present the setting of the second advent of Christ, as well as that of the first advent. Christ came the first time during the Roman period of history; He will come the second time at the climax of the Roman period of the future. This gap is symbolized, in fact, in all four of the visions, as will be seen.

The reason for giving such a predictive survey of history in this time of Daniel is as follows. When God's people were taken captive to Babylonia, it seemed that God was through with them (see Jer. 33:24). This was not true, however, and God desired to let them know this. An effective way to do so was to reveal the nature of future events planned for them. They should know, not only that

they would return from their present captivity, but that they would
in due time experience the coming of their Messiah to deliver them
from spiritual bondage to sin and then much later (in the time of the
restored Roman Empire) from physical bondage to a powerful,
earthly empire, with that deliverance being followed by a powerful
kingdom of their own. God saw fit to reveal this important information through Daniel, an executive in the Babylonian court. This was
a great honor for him.

God's timing for granting this information calls for notice. The
visions were given to Daniel after Nebuchadnezzar had ruled; two
occurred in the early years of Belshazzar and two shortly after the
beginning of the Persian period (see Dan. 7:1; 8:1; 9:1; 10:1). The
visions came, then, toward the close of the captivity period, after the
people had spent most of their time in the foreign land. God, however, had not left the people without any information of this kind
earlier in their captivity; He gave them hope then already. This was
done through the dream given to Nebuchadnezzar, as recorded in
Daniel 2. Actually, this dream was given even before the main
captivity occurred, which means the people had the encouraging information the whole time they were in Babylon.

Symbolism is employed in the visions (especially the first two) as
it was in Nebuchadnezzar's dream. The interpretation of much of the
symbolism is made clear in the text, so that one does not have to
guess. It will be observed that in respect to the predicted events that
have already occurred in history, the visions find a literal, historical
fulfillment; the same should be anticipated, then, in respect to the
events that still lie in the future.

There are two basic differences between the manner in which this
historical preview was presented in Nebuchadnezzar's dream and in
Daniel's initial vision. First, the earlier dream, by presenting one great
image as a whole, having related symbolic parts, pictured the unity
of history running through these empires; however, Daniel's vision,
which presented four distinct beasts, depicted the diversity of history
exhibited by the empires. Second, the humanlike image of the dream
seen by the pagan king represented these empires from man's viewpoint as possessing intrinsic value, corresponding to the value of the
various metals involved; the four beasts seen by the pious Daniel
showed these empires from God's viewpoint as being "beastly" in
nature and value. It should be observed, also, that Daniel's vision
gave greater detail than Nebuchadnezzar's dream, especially concerning events which still lie in the future.

A. The General Setting (Dan. 7:1-3)

A few preliminary matters are first given to provide the setting for the vision. The time of the vision was in Belshazzar's first year, 553 B.C., when Daniel was about sixty-seven years old. Nebuchadnezzar had been dead for nine years, and the kingdom had experienced troubled times since. It would be another fourteen years before the miraculous writing described in chapter 5 would appear on Belshazzar's wall.

In the vision Daniel saw four winds stirring up a great sea. Because the sea regularly symbolizes the nations of the world in Scripture (see Isa. 17:12, 13; 27:1; 57:20; Rev. 17:15), the thought here is that various forces which play on nations were bringing strife and trouble on them. That four winds were involved, apparently blowing from four directions at once, which is contrary to nature, suggests that the world turmoil symbolized was very severe. Then Daniel saw four large animals arise from this sea, not simultaneously but successively. The beasts represented the four successive empires noted, and, since each arose from the sea (nations), the empires were symbolized as being of human origin and nature.

B. The Vision Proper (Dan. 7:4-14)

1. *The three empires (Dan. 7:4-6)*

It is well to treat the first three empires together, for much less is told about them than about the fourth one.

a. Babylonia (Dan. 7:4). The first beast, like a "lion," is symbolic of the empire of Daniel's own day, Babylonia. More specifically, it is symbolic of Nebuchadnezzar, the principal king of this empire. The first beast is unique in this way, for the others all represent empires, not kings. The significance is that in the case of Babylonia, Nebuchadnezzar was unusually important to it, much more so than any one king in the other empires.

The meaning of the symbolism of the lion with eagle's wings is shown by several matters. First, the lion as king of beasts and the eagle as king of birds correspond in importance to the head of gold in Nebuchadnezzar's dream, which was specifically said to represent Nebuchadnezzar (see 2:38). Second, statues of winged lions, believed to represent Nebuchadnezzar and his empire, have been recovered from Babylon's ruins. Third, Daniel's contemporary prophets employed the sign of both the lion and eagle for Nebuchadnezzar (see Jer. 4:7; 49:19, 22; 50:17; Ezek. 17:3; Hab. 1:8). Fourth, the

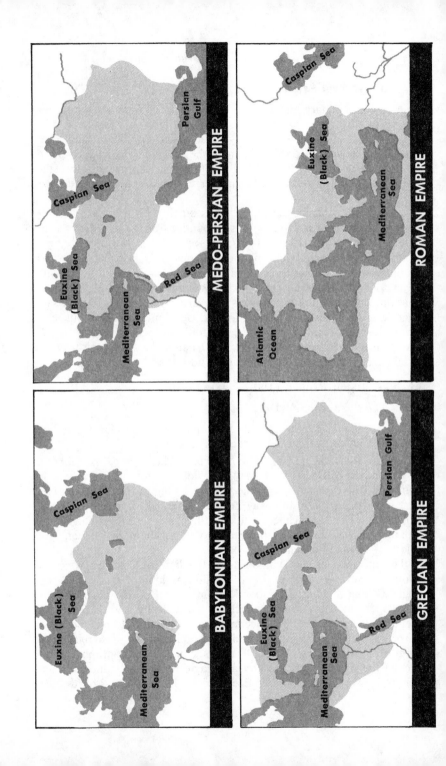

BABYLONIAN EMPIRE

MEDO-PERSIAN EMPIRE

GRECIAN EMPIRE

ROMAN EMPIRE

changes this beast experienced in the vision fit well with the story of Nebuchadnezzar, particularly at the time of his insanity.

The wings being plucked from the lion describes Nebuchadnezzar's power being removed at that time. That the lion was made to stand like a man, with a man's heart being given to it symbolizes Nebuchadnezzar's change of heart on being restored to rationality. He became humbled at that time and much more humanized in his interest toward his subjects rather than "beastly" as before.

b. Medo-Persia (Dan. 7:5). The second beast was like a bear and represents Medo-Persia. It must have this symbolism, for Medo-Persia under Cyrus did succeed Babylonia, as has been seen in the historical section of the book. Also, Medo-Persia was bearlike; it was strong and plodding in its movement rather than swift like the leopard, which was used to symbolize Greece. That the bear was raised up on one side may have two symbolic meanings: first, it may represent the greater importance of the Persian division over the Median (cf. Dan. 8:3); second, it may show that the legs are lifted as if walking and moving ahead; this points to the great Medo-Persian desire for conquest, carried out especially by Cyrus. Then, that it has three ribs in its mouth again represents conquests like a bear having just killed an animal for food. Further, the command "Arise, devour much flesh" points in the same direction. And Medo-Persia did acquire an extensive domain. It became much larger than the Babylonian Empire, stretching finally from Asia Minor to India and as far south as Egypt.

c. Greece (Dan. 7:6). The third beast was like a leopard (or panther) and represents Greece. This symbolism is established by the fact that Greece did destroy and succeed Medo-Persia. Also, its destruction of Medo-Persia was effected with great speed. The leopard is a member of the cat family; it is swift and, as a beast of prey, has an insatiable thirst for blood. The fact, further, that this leopard had four wings on its back speaks also of speed of movement. Under the leadership of Alexander the Great, the borders of Greece were enlarged enormously and with remarkable rapidity, as will be seen more at length in chapter 8.

This leopard also had four heads. Because heads in Scripture normally represent persons or governments, it is logical to take this indication as symbolic of a fourfold division of government, and this is exactly what did occur after Alexander's death. The vast empire he conquered came to be divided among four of his generals, as will also be discussed more in chapter 8. Predictive prophecy involving such detail as this provides significant evidence of scriptural infallibility.

2. The fourth empire (Dan. 7:7, 8)

The fourth beast differed from the others in not being identified by name. Apparently, it did not look like any known animal, probably signifying that no animal was known which could adequately symbolize the empire in view. The beast described in Revelation 13:1-10, commonly taken as parallel in significance to this one, is said to have had features resembling the three animals just noted, the leopard, the bear, and the lion. The significance may be that this fourth beast had characteristics of all three of the prior empires. Its outstanding feature, however, was strength.

a. Rome of past history (Dan. 7:7). The empire symbolized can only be Rome, which historically replaced Greece and which was indeed characterized by strength. Rome reduplicated within itself many of the characteristics of the earlier empires, and it lasted longer than those three put together.[1] The animal is described as being "dreadful and terrible, and strong exceedingly," having "great iron teeth." All this speaks of the strength of Rome, with the teeth being made of the same metal that symbolized the Roman Empire in Nebuchadnezzar's dream. That it "devoured and brake in pieces, and stamped the residue" speaks further of this strength.

b. Rome of future history (Dan. 7:8). The last phrase of verse 7, "it had ten horns," belongs with verse 8. The fact that this beast had ten horns signifies that an extended time-gap must be recognized prior to this indication. This is true for the following reasons.

First, these horns represent ten kings (see Dan. 7:24), which must be contemporaneous in their rule (because the horns exist at the same time and from them grows the "little horn" of verse 8), and there was no time in ancient Rome when ten contemporaneous kings ruled. To find a time for the fulfillment of this symbolism, then, a future time of restoration of the empire must be posited.

Second, any explanation attempting to suit this symbolism in the time of ancient Rome has proven unsatisfactory. The attempt which has most in its favor finds the representation in the numerous small kingdoms into which Rome was broken after its demise as an empire[2]

---

[1]Cf. chap. 2, p. 39.

[2]See Barne's commentary on Daniel, p. 186, for presentation.

and then finds the identity of the little horn in the papal power. This explanation breaks down, however, because ten distinct states, contemporary in time, cannot be identified and also because the Pope has never been parallel in position to kings (as the little horn should be expected to be with other horns); nor did the papacy ever uproot three kings in establishing itself, as was true here of the "little horn (v. 8). It is also significant that the little horn appeared in the vision after the time the ten horns were seen, but the Pope preceded the breakup of Rome into the smaller states.

Third, this beast with its horns was judged by God (called "the Ancient of days") in the vision only after the rise of the little horn (vv. 9-12), and it was after this that a kingdom was given to the Son of man. This sequence fits the thought that this kingdom is Christ's millennial kingdom, which will be established after the judgment of restored Rome and its final king, the little horn, who is properly called the Antichrist. The view that this kingdom is Christ's spiritual kingdom, instituted at His first coming (a view commonly held by those who deny a future Rome), does not fit, for the ancient Roman empire continued long after Christ's first coming and the beginning of His spiritual kingdom.

Fourth, this beast is commonly and correctly identified with the beast of Revelation 17, the symbolism of which further requires a restored Rome. This beast also has ten horns, which represent ten kings (Rev. 17:12). These kings had not yet received power in John's day but would do so along with an eighth beast, which also had not yet appeared (Rev. 17:11). These kings and the beast will appear when they make war with the Lamb, meaning Christ; this occasion corresponds in character to the time when Christ will return to deliver the Jews from the power of this beast and these kings, just prior to the institution of the millennial kingdom (as indicated in chapter 2, p. 41).

An extended gap in time, then, is implied in this vision, as it was in Nebuchadnezzar's dream and again in Daniel's later visions. Today, we live between these two Roman empires. The future form may be quite different from the past; for example, it may be a confederation of European states. But it will still be of empire proportions and will center basically north of the Mediterranean. Rome will be its main city, and there the little horn will become head king.

Verse 8 describes the little horn, which became the center of attention in the vision, as it grew up among the ten original horns. In growing up, it displaced three of those horns, leaving a total of eight.

This implies that though this horn was little when first seen, it became the greatest of all. It must symbolize another king, since it is identified as a horn like the others (cf. vv. 24-26). The last part of the verse says this horn had "eyes like the eyes of a man," apparently indicating both that he will be truly human (and so not a supernatural being of some kind) and that he will possess keen insight. He will also be a boastful person, for the horn had "a mouth speaking great things."

Because the description of this ruler, given both here and in verses 24-26, corresponds to descriptions of the "beast" of Revelation 13:5-8 and 17:11-14, the two are properly identified. The one so described is commonly and correctly called the Antichrist, who will be Satan's counterfeit world ruler, trying to preempt the place of God's true world ruler, Jesus Christ, who will establish His reign during the millennium.

3. God's judgment of future Rome (Dan. 7:9-12)

A judgment scene was depicted next. Thrones were "cast down," meaning they were put in position for service. On the main throne the Ancient of days took His honored seat as judge. This must be God the Father, for in verse 13 He was the one who gave the kingdom to the Son of man. The time in the future when this occasion will be enacted must follow the time of rule of the Antichrist, which means at the close of the great tribulation period, though prior to the establishment of Christ's kingdom. No indication is given as to who occupied the other thrones, but these were probably angels, who do the bidding of God (Heb. 1:14). Perhaps they were not mentioned specifically because they were acting only as passive observers. God alone is Judge. The fact that His hair was described as being white indicates His divine purity; that His throne and its "wheels" were "burning fire" indicates that this was a place of judgment, for fire in Scripture regularly symbolizes judgment (see Exod. 19:18; Deut. 4:24; 9:3; Ps. 18:8; 50:3; Heb. 12:29). The same symbolism is seen in verse 10, in the "fiery stream" mentioned. The huge number of hosts of the verse are angelic beings.

Verse 11 tells of the one who was judged, the beast, who was then "slain and his body destroyed." In other words, in God's judgment on restored Rome, in the future day following the time of the Antichrist's rule, the empire with the little horn as king will be fully done away. This occasion is depicted in Revelation 19:11-21 as occurring when Christ comes in power and destroys the army of the Antichrist (called "the beast" in Rev. 19:20), casting him and his helper, the false prophet, directly into the lake of fire, meaning hell.

Verse 12 tells of the end of the first three beasts — the lion (Babylon), the bear (Medo-Persia), and the leopard (Greece). The vision earlier revealed their existence, but said nothing regarding their cessation. This is dealt with by the words, "their dominion was taken away." The further indication that "their lives were prolonged for a season and time" is best understood in the following sense: These three earlier empires each continued to exist in a manner, after the time when they had ceased to exist in name, in that their people and cultures were absorbed into their respective successors. The reason for mentioning this here is that the situation will be different in respect to the fourth empire in its restored form. It will not be absorbed in a parallel way into the new empire established by Christ, for His empire will be entirely different, new, and perfectly righteous in all aspects.

4. *Christ's millennial kingdom (Dan. 7:13, 14)*

The same court scene continued in verses 13 and 14. The identity of the one who came to stand before the great Judge, however, changed. He was called "the Son of man," meaning Christ. He was brought, presumably by angels, up to the Ancient of days, and pronouncement was given; but how different it was from that voiced earlier. No penalty was meted out this time; instead "there was given him dominion, and glory, and a kingdom, that all people, nations, and languages, should serve him." This kingdom will not "pass away" or "be destroyed" like the four kingdoms before His. The kingdom in view is of course the glorious millennial kingdom of Christ, which will come to existence after the restored Roman rule under the Antichrist has been judged and destroyed.

C. The Interpretation (Dan. 7:15-28)

With the vision proper narrated, Daniel presented its interpretation, though really this, too, was a part of the vision, for the explanation was given by one "that stood by," meaning an angel.

1. *Explanation in general (Dan. 7:15-18)*

The first part of the explanation concerns a general interpretation of the overall vision. The entire explanation was given, as noted, by "one of them that stood by," no doubt meaning an angel, still seen in vision form. Daniel asked this one the meaning of what he had seen, and he responded with the general explanation. The four beasts were four "kings" or kingdoms that would arise, but in due time the "saints of the most High" would become supreme in the earth, and they would "possess the kingdom for ever," a reference to the kingdom just indicated as given to Christ.

2. Explanation of the fourth beast (Dan. 7:19-28)

Having heard this general explanation, Daniel asked more specifically regarding the fourth beast and especially the ten horns and the other one which came up among them, which was "more stout" than they were (vv. 19, 20). Then Daniel added a note omitted in the earlier report of the vision. He said that he had seen this later-arising horn make war with the saints and prevail over them, "until the Ancient of days came, and judgment was given to the saints . . . and the time came that the saints possessed the kingdom." This note fits exactly into what has been seen: the Antichrist will rule until made to cease by God, and then Christ's millennial reign will begin. In other words, the false ruler of Satan will be deposed in favor of God's true ruler. During this time of the false ruler's reign, the saints (those who remain faithful to God) will be persecuted, and this will continue until God brings judgment on the Antichrist and installs His own Son as true world ruler. The saints in view here are undoubtedly those depicted in Revelation 7:9-17, commonly called tribulation saints, and saved Jews of Israel, mentioned in Revelation 7:1-8 and 14:1-5.

The angelic messenger replied to Daniel that the fourth beast was a fourth kingdom (Rome) and that its ten horns represented ten kings from which another would arise (vv. 23, 24). Then he continued to give information about this later one (the little horn, the Antichrist). This one would "speak great words against the most High," meaning against God; he would "wear out the saints," a reference to the persecution just noted; and he would try to "change times and laws," meaning the natural laws of God which pertain especially to seasons and time schedules. Something of the latter was attempted during the French Revolution, when a ten-day work-week was unsuccessfully tried.

The power of this false ruler would last for "a time and times and the dividing of time" (v. 25). This formula for a specific period means three-and-a-half years. This follows from the fact that the use of a singular (time), a plural (times), and a "dividing" (half) of times makes sense only if used in reference to a total of three and a half of some unit of time; in other contexts, the equivalent of this formula is identified as three-and-a-half years (see Dan. 12:7; Rev. 12:14; cf. 12:6). Further, the idea of three-and-a-half years fits the duration of the last half of the seven-year tribulation period, which, as will be seen in chapter 9, is the exact time when the Antichrist will enjoy the height of his power.

Verses 26 and 27 speak again of the judgment time of the Antichrist (cf. vv. 9-11), followed by the inauguration of Christ's rule, when the saints will be in control. Once more it is said that this kingdom will be everlasting, in contrast, as has been seen, to the four earlier kingdoms.

The last verse merely closes the entire vision. The angel's final words are first given: "Hitherto is the end of the matter." Then Daniel stated that his thoughts were much troubled as a result of all that he had seen and heard. Momentous matters had been presented, with kingdoms rising, persecutions ensuing, punishments resulting, and a final ruling of saints. All this was too much for Daniel to absorb and understand at one time. But though distressed by all this information, Daniel did not put it away from his mind; rather he pondered it, no doubt trying to figure out what it all meant. One must remember that Daniel lived before any of the predicted matters occurred. Looking back now, it is possible to see quite clearly those aspects already fulfilled, but they would have been puzzling then. They all came to pass exactly as predicted, however, whether understood by Daniel or not; and those pertaining to events still future will be fulfilled just as exactly, whether we today understand them fully or not.

For Further Study

1. Read articles in a Bible dictionary or encyclopedia on: (a) animals of the Bible, noting the lion, bear, and leopard, (b) Antichrist, (c) Millennium.
2. Identify each of the empires symbolized by the four animals seen by Daniel.
3. In what way do the ten horns of the fourth beast give evidence that the Roman confederacy will be restored?
4. Characterize the person symbolized by the little horn.
5. Characterize the scene of judgment of Daniel 7:9-11.
6. Contrast the scene as set forth in Daniel 7:13, 14.
7. List the things said about Christ's millennial kingdom in this chapter.

Chapter 8

The Second Vision: Antiochus Epiphanes

The interest now turns to Daniel's second vision, which concerns a part of the sweep of time covered in the first. That part involves the Medo-Persian and Grecian empires, with emphasis on the rise of a despicable ruler, Antiochus Epiphanes, during the Greek Empire. Once more animals are used for symbolism, but in place of the lion and bear employed in the first vision for these two empires, a two-horned ram and a one-horned goat appear. The ruler, Antiochus Epiphanes, is symbolized by the figure of a little horn, as the Antichrist was in the first vision. The reason for this identity is that this person of Old Testament time acted in much the same way toward the Jewish people as the Antichrist will in the future time. He was the antichrist of Old Testament time, who prefigured the true Antichrist of the last days.

Notice that the language used in this and following chapters of Daniel reverts to Hebrew, rather than continuing further with Aramaic, which was employed from Daniel 2:4 on.[1]

A. The General Setting (Dan. 8:1, 2)

The general setting of the vision is again given first. The date of the vision is indicated as being the third year of Belshazzar, which means two years after the first vision (see 7:1), or 551 B.C., when Daniel was about sixty-nine. In contrast to the former vision, which came at night, this one seems to have come in the daytime, for no mention of night or sleep is made. In the vision, Daniel saw himself in "Shushan . . . in the province of Elam . . . by the river of Ulai." It is quite clear that he was not actually there but only saw himself there in vision. Shushan (called Susa by the Greeks) was a city about 230 miles east of Babylon (where Daniel lived) and 120 miles

[1]See Introduction for discussion of the significance of the language change.

north of the Persian Gulf. At the time of Daniel's vision, Shushan was merely an important eastern city, but earlier it had been the capital of Elam, and after Daniel's time, it became one of the royal cities of the Medo-Persian Empire (see Neh. 1:1; Esther 1:2). The Ulai River here mentioned is known classically as the Eulaeus River and is best identified with an artificial canal, about nine hundred feet wide, which passed close to Shushan on the northeast.

B. The Vision Proper (Dan. 8:3-14)

1. *The two-horned ram: Medo-Persia (Dan. 8:3-4)*

A ram the first of the two symbolic animals of the vision, is introduced immediately. Verse 20 definitely identifies the ram as Medo-Persia. Daniel saw the animal standing by the Ulai River, having two horns, but one was higher and it came up after the shorter one. The significance is clear. Media was already a major power when Persia was only a minor province to the south. However, on coming to power in Persia, Cyrus succeeded in gaining control over powerful Media (c. 550 B.C.) and then made his own country the more important of the two. With these combined, he moved on to establish the vast Medo-Persian domain.

Daniel saw the ram push "westward and northward and southward" signifying that Cyrus, as ruler of this combined power, would conquer widely, especially in these three directions. This did happen, as Cyrus marched his army all the way into Asia Minor, going westward; then later he seized extensive land toward both the north and south. Some territory was also taken toward the east, but not a significant amount. That no beast was able to "stand before him" indicates that Cyrus would do all this with remarkable ease, which also proved true. He experienced little real opposition in his wide conquests.

2. *The one-horned goat: Greece (Dan. 8:5-8)*

Daniel now saw a second animal, the one-horned goat. Verse 21 identifies it as Greece. It came from the west (Greece was to the west of Medo-Persia), without touching the ground (indicating great speed). The goat "had a notable horn between his eyes," which symbolized the "first king" (v. 21), namely, Alexander the Great. He was not the first king of Greece itself, of course, but was the first ruler of the great empire. Daniel then saw the goat attack the ram, which previously had been so successful, and defeat him completely.

Alexander crossed the Hellespont and moved into the Persian territory of Asia Minor in 334 B.C., when he was just twenty-one years old. He led approximately thirty-five thousand men. He joined in battle with the Persians shortly after the crossing and soundly defeated them at the Granicus River. A year later he met the Persians in the battle of Issus, at the eastern extreme of Asia Minor in the Taurus Mountains, and won again. Then he turned southward with his troops and captured the entire eastern Mediterranean seaboard, including Tyre, which he took after building his famous causeway out to the island on which the city then stood. From there he moved on into northeast Africa and took Egypt. Then he turned back into Palestine and moved on to the headwaters of the Tigris River, where a great battle with the Persians was fought in 331 B.C., and for the third time he defeated this foe. All three times he was outnumbered, but all three times he won by better-planned and better-executed strategy. With the third and final battle won, the entire Medo-Persian domain lay before him for the taking, and he did take it, marching his army all the way to India, south down the Indus River, and then back to Babylon. In twelve years, he conquered all the Medo-Persian territory and then wept that there were no more worlds to conquer. This truly was speed of conquest, symbolized here by the swift-moving goat and, in the first vision, by the leopard with four wings.

Verse 8 states that when the he-goat was strong, the "great horn" was broken. On returning to Babylon, Alexander was taken with a severe fever, and in June of 323 B.C. he died at the age of thirty-two. Had his earlier life not been one of drunkenness and debauchery, he might have thrown off the attack. As it was, however, he was taken in death, a young military genius cut off at the height of achievement and power.

Then Daniel saw "four notable" horns grow up in place of the broken one. The thought here parallels the four heads of Daniel 7:6. Alexander's empire was divided among four of his generals: Cassander receiving Macedonia and Greece; Lysimachus, Thrace and much of Asia Minor; Seleucus, Syria and a vast region to the east; and Ptolemy, Egypt. For a while a fifth general, Antigonus, held territory in Asia Minor, but in 301 B.C. he was overthrown and killed. Nothing in the symbolism indicates that Alexander himself thus divided the empire, and he did not. In fact, the divisions came only after extensive fighting among the generals over a period of about twenty-two years.

3. *The emergence of a little horn: Antiochus Epiphanes*
   (Dan. 8:9-14)

   a. The appearance (Dan. 8:9). Out of one of these four new horns Daniel now saw "a little horn" grow. It was small at first, but like the "little horn" in the first vision, it soon became very strong, conquering toward the south, the east, and "the pleasant land" (Palestine). As noted, this horn symbolizes Antiochus Epiphanes, who was the eighth king after Seleucus, the general who received the Syrian division of the empire. Antiochus ascended the throne following the murder of his brother Seleucus Philopator, the former king. The king's son, Demetrius, was the rightful heir to the throne, but he was held hostage in Rome at the time. As a result, Antiochus Epiphanes, through flattery and bribes (see Dan. 11:21), was able to seize the throne for himself. Thus, he did begin small, since he was not even the rightful heir, but having achieved the rule, he asserted himself with vigor and made rather extensive conquests, giving special attention to Palestine, "the pleasant land."

   b. His outrageous activity (Dan. 9:10-12). The manner in which Antiochus became "great toward" Palestine was presented next. Daniel saw the little horn become strong, even against "the host of heaven," meaning the stars (Jer. 33:22), which here represent the people of God in Palestine (cf. Gen. 15:5; 22:17; Exod. 12:41; Dan. 12:3). The thought is that Antiochus would begin to oppress God's people, the Jews (see v. 24). Then he was seen to cast the stars to the ground, meaning that he would kill many of them. History records that he did indeed do this, killing about 100,000 Jews.

   Verse 11 says that "he magnified himself even to the prince of the host." The reference here is to God Himself, and not merely to an earthly leader like the high priest of the day (named Onias), for verse 25 identifies this one as "Prince of princes." [2] Antiochus did this by doing away with the "daily sacrifice" and casting down "the place of his sanctuary." The Hebrew word translated "daily sacrifice" means that which is "continual," and here designates whatever was regular in the temple ceremonies. The record of Antiochus' atrocities is given in the apocryphal books of 1 and 2 Maccabees. For instance 1 Maccabees 1:44-50 reads:

   > And the king [Antiochus] sent letters by messengers unto Jerusalem and the cities of Judah, that they should follow the foreign

---

[2] It will be observed under verse 25 that the main reference is to the Antichrist, but a secondary reference is carried to Antiochus, making the evidence valid.

customs of the land, and keep burnt offerings, and sacrifices, and
drink offerings, out of the sanctuary; and that they should pro-
fane sabbaths and festival days; and pollute the sanctuary and
priests; build altars, and groves and idol temples, and sacrifice
swine's flesh, and unclean animals; that they should also leave
their sons uncircumcised, make their souls abominable with all
manner of uncleanness and profanation; to the end that they
might forget the law, and change all the ordinances.[3]

Verse 12 indicates further that this decree was indeed carried out.
The Hebrew of the verse is difficult to translate literally, but the
meaning is clear: Antiochus perverted the sacrifices and then caused
them to cease, thus casting truth to the ground. Outwardly, he
appeared to prosper and succeed in all that he attempted to do in this
way. Certainly, people of the day wondered why God would allow
this man to do such terrible things to the people of God and to the
very Temple of God. It was not for them to question, however, even
as it never has been for any of God's children.

  c. *Duration of persecution (Dan. 8:13, 14).* Daniel's vision now
revealed how long this time of suffering would last. He heard one
"saint" (angel) speaking; then another was heard to ask the first
one how long the time would be. The answer was, "Unto two thousand and three hundred days." The Hebrew words translated "days"
mean literally, "evening-mornings." The thought is that there would
be twenty-three hundred "evening-mornings" before these atrocities
would end.

  Though various interpretations have been made of this number,
the correct one is the most obvious. Antiochus would continue his
devastations on Jerusalem for a total of twenty-three hundred days, or
about six-and-one-third years. Considering the history of Antiochus
Epiphanes in his relation to the Jews, this period of time fits very well.
The verse indicates that the period would close with the cleansing
or restoration of the Temple. This occurred in December 165 B.C.
under the leadership of Judas Maccabeus. If we figure back from
this date, the twenty-three hundred days bring us to September 171
B.C., which should be, then, the month when an event of sufficient
significance occurred to mark it as the beginning of Antiochus' anti-
Jewish activities. Though the identity of that particular event is not
known (for lack of adequate history of the time), it is clear that the
year 171 B.C. did see the beginning of these atrocities, and such an

  [3]This is the author's own translation. For similar passages, see 1 Macc.
1:16-19, 29-32, 52-61; 2 Macc. 6:1-11, 18-31; 7:1-42.

event could well have occurred in September of that year. Until 171 B.C. peaceful relations had existed between Antiochus and the Jews. Beginning with that year, however, a series of events transpired, involving especially the Jewish high priesthood, which prompted severe measures by Antiochus.[4]

C. The Vision Interpreted (Dan. 8:15-27)

Like the pattern of chapter 7, the last half of this chapter is given to the interpretation of the vision of the first half. It follows the pattern further by having the interpretation supplied by a heavenly messenger, so that in effect the vision still continued, though with a change of scene.

1. Gabriel the interpreter (Dan. 8:15-19)

When the vision was completed, Daniel still saw himself at the Ulai River, longing to know the meaning. Then a person having the appearance of a man suddenly stood before him to give that meaning. At the same time, Daniel heard a voice from above the river (as if between its banks, apparently) telling this one to reveal it. The voice must have been from God Himself, and the one seen by Daniel was then called by his name, Gabriel.

The angel Gabriel is identified twice in Daniel — here and in 9:21. He is also mentioned twice in Luke (1:19, 26). One other angel is similarly named in Scripture; that is Michael, called the archangel (Jude 9). Daniel also mentioned Michael (10:13, 21; 12:1). Scripture presents Michael as the chief of the angels and Gabriel as the head communicator of the divine message. In Daniel's vision Gabriel is seen in this role.

Gabriel approached Daniel, and Daniel became extremely fearful and fell upon his face. It is normal for mortals to experience fear in the presence of the supernatural (cf. Judg. 6:22, 23; Job 42:5, 6; Isa. 6:1-5). A sense of personal sinfulness becomes overpowering in the presence of perfect holiness. Gabriel's manner of response was reassuring to the fallen man, however. He did not speak of any sin on Daniel's part but just began to carry out the divine order. He did so by speaking first about the meaning of the vision in general, stating that it concerned "the time of the end."

Daniel's emotional involvement became more than he could stand, for it is stated that he fell into "a deep sleep," meaning, quite clearly,

[4]See later discussion under Dan. 11:21-23.

that he fainted. Gabriel, however, touched him and restored him to consciousness. Then he told him again that he was about to speak of "what shall be in the last end of the indignation."

The word "indignation" carries a double reference. It refers certainly to God's time of judgment on Israel at the time of Antiochus Epiphanes; but it refers also to God's future time of judgment during the great tribulation, in the last half of which the little horn of Daniel's first vision will bring even worse affliction.[5] In this double reference, Antiochus is typical of the little horn (Antichrist).

2. *Preliminary explanations (Dan. 8:20-22)*

Gabriel then began to give the explanation of the vision. He did so by noting, first, matters we have already observed: that the two-horned goat symbolized "the kings of Media and Persia"; that the one-horned goat symbolized "the king of Greece," with its one horn representing "the first king"; and that the four horns which replaced the one great broken horn symbolized four kingdoms that would arise, "but not in his power." The ram and goat are said to symbolize the kings of Medo-Persia and Greece, respectively, rather than the countries themselves; but this should not be taken as significant. The reference must be either to all the kings of these empires, taken collectively, or else, in a figurative sense, to the countries themselves. Actually kings and kingdoms are closely intertwined in thought in both the first and second visions.

The meaning of the phrase "but not in his power" is that none of the generals who took over as leaders of the succeeding four divisions of Alexander's empire ruled with the same power as he did. This does not mean that they were especially weak, but only that they did not measure up to him. Alexander was one of the truly strong leaders of history. He kept his army together during approximately twelve years while they were continually away from home, until he had conquered the greatest amount of territory ever controlled by one ruler.

3. *A double prediction (Dan. 8:23-25)*

a. *Two persons predicted (Dan. 8:23).* Gabriel then began to describe the little horn who would come. He did so in language which often finds fulfillment in Antiochus Epiphanes, the little horn of this chapter and of ancient time; but at other times it goes beyond what that person did and, therefore, must be in reference to the little

[5]For further discussions, see L. J. Wood, *A Commentary on Daniel*, pp. 222-224.

horn of chapter 7 and of future history. That similar language should be applicable to both is perfectly reasonable, as already indicated, since one was typical of the other. It is important to recognize that Antiochus was typical of the Antichrist, for an important source of information regarding the Antichrist is thus made available. One need only study the actions of Antiochus, and he can know, at least in general, what the actions of the Antichrist will be. In considering what Gabriel had to say in describing these persons, it will be helpful to note which aspects pertain especially to Antiochus and which to the Antichrist.

The indication of verse 23 that "in the latter time of their king-dom" this one would "stand up" can well be applied to Antiochus. Antiochus came to power toward the close of the Grecian period (actually 175-164 B.C.). The next phrase, however, which indicates that this would occur "when the transgressors are come to the full" (meaning when sin has abounded so much that God's mercy can no longer ignore it) is language not otherwise used of Antiochus' time. It is significantly employed, however, in respect to the days of the great tribulation, when the Antichrist will rule (see Matt. 23:32; Luke 18:7, 8; 1 Thess. 2:16; 2 Tim. 3:1-9).

Verse 23 further describes this person as "a king of fierce coun-tenance, and understanding dark sentences." The word translated "fierce" basically means "strong, vehement." The word for "dark sentences" (riddles) means "something twisted, involved." The thought is that this king will be fierce and cruel in manner, but, at the same time, capable of solving difficult problems of his kingdom. Some expositors understand the latter aspect to include "tactics of deception," which is quite possible. However, the basic thought of the word used is made clear in Daniel 5:12, where it refers to Daniel. There it definitely means the ability to solve difficult problems. Anti-ochus qualifies in respect to cruelty and deceit, as will also the Anti-christ, but he was not particularly clever in solving difficult problems, as the Antichrist will be.

b. Their work (Dan. 8:24, 25). Gabriel now continued by speak-ing of the work of the king in view. He said first that this king will be "mighty, but not by his own power." Antiochus was a mighty ruler, but not outstandingly so; his own father, Antiochus III (see Dan. 11:10-19) was probably stronger. The Antichrist, however, will become extremely powerful as a world figure in his day. Also, the fact of being strong "not by his own power" fits the Antichrist much better. He will be empowered especially by Satan to serve as

Satan's counterfeit world ruler (see Rev. 13:2). No doubt Satan was behind the rise of Antiochus, too, but this is never stated explicitly, as it is regarding the Antichrist.

Further, this one will "destroy wonderfully." The Hebrew word translated "wonderfully" means something separate and unique. This person, then, will destroy in a unique, distinct manner. This idea fits well with the thought of 2 Thessalonians 2:9 that the "man of sin," the Antichrist, would be empowered by Satan to perform "signs and lying wonders." Further, this one will "prosper, and practice, and shall destroy the mighty and the holy people." It is true that this language fits the work of Antiochus, but again it uniquely suits descriptions of the Antichrist, as for instance in Revelation 13:7: "And it was given him to make war with the saints, and to overcome them: and power was given him over all kindreds, and tongues, and nations."

In verse 25, Gabriel says that this one will "cause craft to prosper; . . . and he shall magnify himself . . . and by peace shall destroy many." In other words, he will be proud and practice deceit and do this by showing himself peaceful and then bringing destruction instead. The language fits both persons. Antiochus surely was proud, and he did use deceit to achieve the kingship and later in his atrocities against the Jews (see 1 Maccabees 1:29-32). The Antichrist, too, will be very proud and make extensive use of deceptive tactics (see Dan. 7:8, 25; 2 Thess. 2:4; Rev. 13:5, 6).

Still further, this one "shall also stand up against the Prince of princes." In verse 11, Antiochus was seen magnifying himself against the "prince of the host," who was identified as God. However, this phrase, "Prince of princes," is quite different. It does carry a secondary reference to the previous phrase, but it fits much better the pattern of the titles, "Lord of lords" and "King of kings" (cf. 1 Tim. 6:15; Rev. 1:5; 17:14; 19:16), which are regularly ascribed to Christ. This suggests that the principal one here in mind is Christ, meaning that the person mainly in view as opposing Him must be the Antichrist. In the manner of Antiochus' disdain for God, then, the Antichrist will seek to stand against Christ when Christ comes in power to bring vengeance on him (cf. 2 Thess. 1:8; Rev. 19:19).

Lastly, this one will "be broken without hand." The thought is that no human hand would be involved in this person's death. This came true in a sense regarding Antiochus, for, as stated in 1 Maccabees 6:8-16, he died of grief and remorse in Babylon. He had just been defeated at Elymais in Persia, after which he heard other disheartening news from his home area; he was not able to bear the shock of this all at once. Human hands were involved in his death indirectly, however, in that they brought about the reasons for all the bad news he received. But no man's hand will be involved in the breaking of the Antichrist. His army will be destroyed by the sharp sword from Christ's mouth, and he himself will be cast alive into the lake of fire at the time of Christ's coming in power to deliver His people (Rev. 19:20, 21; cf. Dan. 7:26; 11:45).

4. *Importance of the vision (Dan. 8:26, 27)*

As a way of stressing the importance and reliability of the vision, Gabriel closed by saying that it was indeed true. Then he directed Daniel to "shut . . . up the vision" (so as to preserve it), since the fulfillment would not be "for many days." The thought is that people of later time would need the instruction and comfort it contained, so care should be used to preserve and guard it securely.

The statement that Daniel "fainted, and was sick certain days" stresses further the importance of the vision. He had fainted during the vision, but then was soon revived; this fainting now left him ill for many days. The significance seems to be that Daniel was emotionally affected by this vision more than any of the others. After recovery he returned to the work that he was then doing for the king (probably not as head of the wise men, as noted in chapter 5, but nevertheless something important), but he still remained "astonished at the vision." The phrase, "but none understood it" could mean that others to whom Daniel told the vision did not understand it. However, it probably refers to Daniel himself. He had heard Gabriel's words, but all their significances were not clear. He evidently continued to turn the thoughts over in his mind for many days.

For Further Study

1. Read articles in a Bible dictionary or encyclopedia on: (a) Alexander the Great, (b) Antiochus Epiphanes.
2. What do the two horns of the ram symbolize?
3. Identify and date the three battles in which Alexander crushed the Persians.
4. Identify and characterize the person symbolized by the little horn of Daniel 8:9.
5. To what do the twenty-three hundred days of Daniel 8:14 refer?
6. Identify which aspects of Daniel 8:23-25 refer primarily to Antiochus Epiphanes and which to the Antichrist.

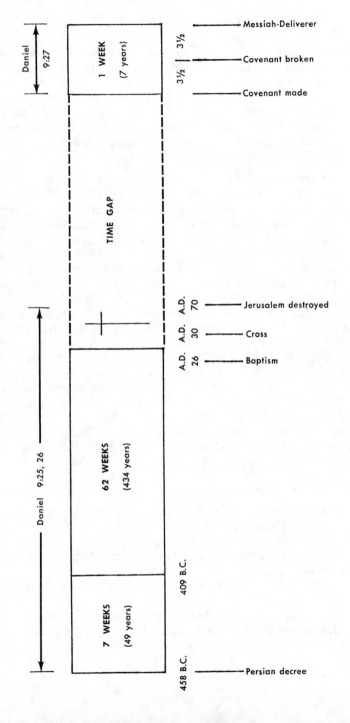

SEVENTY WEEKS OF DANIEL

Daniel 9:27

1 WEEK
(7 years)

3½ — Messiah-Deliverer
3½ — Covenant broken
3½ — Covenant made

TIME GAP

Daniel 9:25, 26

A.D. 70 — Jerusalem destroyed
A.D. 30 — Cross
A.D. 26 — Baptism

62 WEEKS
(434 years)

7 WEEKS
(49 years)

409 B.C.

458 B.C. — Persian decree

Chapter 9

The Third Vision: The Seventy Weeks

Chapter 9 is divided into two parts. The first nineteen verses present a prayer by Daniel that the captivity of Judah might soon come to an end. It was prompted by his notice of Jeremiah's prediction that the captivity would last 70 years, and at that time almost 70 years had passed since the occasion when he and his friends had been taken captive. The last eight verses of the chapter concern God's response to the prayer, given again through the angel Gabriel. The response centers in the prediction that 70 "weeks" of years (490 years) were planned for God's people during which various matters would be accomplished on their behalf.

The appearance of Gabriel in this instance may have been in real, corporeal form, rather than in a vision, as in chapter 8. If so, this time of revelation should not be classed as a vision, strictly speaking, but as an actual face-to-face communication (see Dan. 9:20). If it was merely a vision, the occasion still was quite different from the first two visions, for the only feature in it was Gabriel himself speaking to Daniel.

The main importance of the information communicated concerns the last "week" of the total seventy. An extended time-lapse occurs just prior to this seventieth week, in parallel with the time-lapse noted in Nebuchadnezzar's first dream and Daniels' two earlier visions. Therefore, whereas the first sixty-nine weeks were completed at the time of Christ's first coming, the seventieth will only be completed just before His second coming, and it will constitute the seven-year period called the great tribulation.

A. The General Setting (Dan. 9:1, 2)

Once more Daniel began by dating the revelation. It was the first year of Darius who, as seen in chapter 6, was made to rule over Babylon by Cyrus in late 539 B.C., making his first year 538 B.C.

111

About thirteen years had elapsed, then, since the second vision, and Daniel was now about eighty-two. Darius' father, here called Ahasuerus, was not the same man who took Esther to wife (Esther 1:1), for that time followed this occasion by fifty years.

Daniel stressed the time as the first year of Darius' reign by repeating the fact in verse 2. The significance is that, through his reading in Jeremiah (see Jer. 25:11, 12; 29:10), he knew that the time of the captivity should be drawing to a close. Babylon had fallen, Medo-Persia was in power (as he himself had seen predicted in the earlier visions), and the seventy years foretold by Jeremiah had nearly elapsed. He did not see any indications that suggested the return to Jerusalem was about to take place, and so he came now to ask God to be pleased to work to that end.

B. The Prayer (Dan. 9:3-19)

Burdened for his countrymen, Daniel began to pray. Surprisingly, though his interest was in an early return of the people, he did not make this the stress of his prayer. In fact, he mentioned this request specifically only at the very last, with the words "defer not." His emphasis, rather, was on the sin of the people, making earnest confession of the sin before God. Daniel clearly was fearful lest this sin should cause God to postpone the return; Daniel recognized that the greatest need was in seeking God's forgiveness, rather than in presenting the request proper.

1. *Daniel's attitude in prayer (Dan. 9:3, 4)*

Attitude in prayer is always important. The "how" of prayer is more a matter of attitude than of words. Prayer must come from the heart. Words which issue from the heart are only the fruit of what God has already seen within. Verses 3 and 4 say much about Daniel's attitude.

First, Daniel set his "face unto the Lord." This suggests definite purpose on his part. He prayed because he felt the need to pray. He had a burden that had to be expressed. Then he sought God through "prayer and supplications." The first word means "intercession" and the second, "entreaty for mercy." Daniel was coming humbly, beseeching God to show favor. This humility was further emphasized by "fasting, and sackcloth, and ashes." Daniel clearly had made preparation for this time of prayer; he had fasted and then come to pray dressed in sackcloth, with ashes sprinkled on his head.

All three matters symbolized contriteness of heart (see Ezra 8:23; Neh. 9:1; Esther 4:1, 3, 16; Job 2:12; Jonah 3:5, 6). God gives ear to the penitent heart.

Daniel finally began his prayer in verse 4, though here, too, there are indications regarding his attitude of heart. First he spoke of making his confession. Actually, he was about to make confession for Israel, but he identified himself with the people. Then Daniel rendered glory to God, speaking of His greatness and His mercy to those "that love him, and . . . keep his commandments." God is pleased with praise of this kind. Here it showed Daniel's attitude of heart in respect to being thankful before God.

It should be mentioned that in this chapter Daniel referred to God by His special name "Yahweh" (rendered "Lord" in the King James Version and "Jehovah" in the American Standard Version). The name is used hundreds of times throughout the Old Testament, but in Daniel it is found only in this chapter, where it is used seven times. It is God's name of grace and condescension, used in contexts of revelation and prayer. It is particularly appropriate in this chapter because of the lengthy prayer Daniel offered.

2. *Daniel's confession (Dan. 9:5-11a)*

Then Daniel began to present his confession. He did so by using four parallel verbs which stressed the thought of Israel's sinfulness. Israel had "sinned," "committed iniquity," "done wickedly," and "rebelled." Then he summarized the thought of all four by saying that the people had departed from God's precepts and judgments. The people had not been obeying God's will. In verse 6, he became more specific, saying that the people had not listened to God's servants, the prophets, who had brought their messages to Israel's "kings," "princes," and "fathers" and to "all the people." God had tried to give warning of impending judgment, but the people had not taken heed. As a result (vv. 7, 8), Daniel said, "shame of face" (a better translation than "confusion of faces") belonged to Israel, in contrast to the perfect righteousness of God. This shame applied to all Israelites, whether in captivity with Daniel, or still in Jerusalem, or wherever they might be. This shame consisted of the punishment that was then being experienced, and it was true for everyone, including "kings," "princes," and the "fathers."

In verses 9 to 11a, Daniel referred to the "mercies and forgivenesses" God extended in spite of Israel's failure to walk in God's laws as set before the people by "his servants the prophets." Daniel was clearly awed by this remarkable response of God. What grace God had bestowed when His people had been so undeserving!

3. *Recognized retribution (Dan. 9:11b-14)*

In the middle of verse 11, Daniel began to speak of the just retribution God brought on Israel for this sin. Daniel wanted to stress his recognition that God was just and righteous in His present punishment of the people. Daniel was not complaining, then; rather, he acknowledged God's justice in the hope that the people would repent. This should always be the attitude of God's children in time of discipline. Daniel stated, "Therefore the curse is poured upon us, and the oath that is written in the law of Moses." In other words, what God had warned about in past history was now being experienced. There was no reason to be surprised at this discipline, therefore; it had to be accepted by the people as their just due (cf. Lev. 26:14-39; Deut. 27:15-26; 28:15-68).

Then in verse 12 Daniel restated the idea another way. God had "confirmed his words, which he spake against us, and against our judges" (general term here for Israel's leaders). The "great evil" mentioned is obviously the captivity then being experienced. Verse 13 adds the thought that, though God had sent this punishment, still Israel would not listen to His voice and turn from their sin. In verse 14, Daniel reiterated the thought by saying that God had "watched upon [literally, "kept in store"] the evil" (the captivity) to use it as it was then being experienced, because of Israel's past disobedience. Daniel was careful to state that God was "righteous in all" this disciplinary activity.

4. *Request for mercy (Dan. 9:15, 16)*

Then Daniel turned to the matter of asking for God's mercy. Sin had been confessed and retribution recognized; it was now appropriate to make petition. Daniel based his plea on the fact that God had been merciful many years before when He had brought Israel out of Egypt. God had done this with His all-sufficient mighty hand and had thereby achieved renown for Himself. Daniel desired that God would be similarly merciful now, in turning His anger and fury from His city Jerusalem. Because of the present condition, God's people had become a reproach among the neighboring pagans, who accordingly thought ill of the God Israel worshiped; therefore, Daniel implied, God would again achieve renown if He would extend mercy in delivering His people. This would make these neighbors realize that Israel's God was great and powerful after all. It is evident that Daniel wanted to make clear that his first interest was in God's honor, rather than in the earthly benefit of his people.

5. *Request for deliverance (Dan. 9:17-19)*

Finally, Daniel voiced his request for Israel's deliverance. He had worked gradually toward it and at last made it. In verse 17 he approached it only indirectly. He asked that God show favor toward His sanctuary (in Jerusalem) that had lain desolate all the years of Israel's captivity. In this condition it was not a cause for honor to God; therefore, God's own interest once more would be served if the people were permitted to return to it. In verse 18, Daniel asked God to look down upon the sad condition of the captives in Babylon as well as on the city of Jerusalem. He implied that if God would do this, He would be influenced to permit the desired return. Once more, however, Daniel was quick to add that he was not asking this because Israel deserved the consideration.

It is in verse 19 that Daniel made the direct petition. With evident emotion, he requested that God "hear," "forgive," "hearken and do," and "defer not." With the last two words, the request was voiced. Daniel had waited till this point of climax to bring it. He did not want God to "defer" His time schedule. This plea must be seen in the light of the three periods of Israel's captivity (see Introduction). Daniel and his three friends had been taken in 605 B.C., a second contingent (ten thousand craftsmen) in 591 B.C., and the main group in 586 B.C. The seventy years predicted by Jeremiah were nearly concluded if the beginning date was 605 B.C., but it would be proportionately removed in time if either of the other two dates were employed. Accordingly, what Daniel was really requesting was that God would be pleased not to choose either of the later dates as the starting point for the seventy years rather than Daniel's time of captivity, 605 B.C.

C. The Prediction of the Seventy Weeks (Dan. 9:20-27)

God's response to Daniel, given through the angel Gabriel, came even before the prophet finished the prayer. The content of the response no doubt surprised him, for it did not refer to the seventy-year captivity at all. It spoke rather of a period of time called "seventy weeks," which had been determined for the accomplishment of certain matters relative to God's people. Numerous interpretations for these weeks have been proposed by expositors, but the one presented here agrees with the interpretation already set forth regarding Nebuchadnezzar's dream and Daniel's earlier visions.

1. *Gabriel appears once more (Dan. 9:20-23)*

Verse 20 says that Daniel was interrupted in his prayer by the appearance of Gabriel. Gabriel may have timed his arrival at the moment Daniel came to the completion of what he had intended to say, or Daniel may simply have stopped when the great angel made his presence known. In verse 21 Daniel referred to Gabriel as the one he had seen in the earlier vision, but it should be remembered that thirteen years had elapsed. The verse also says that Gabriel arrived by flying swiftly. Because of this phrase and the fact that the angels of Isaiah's earlier vision are said to have had six wings (Isa. 6:2), the idea has arisen that all angels have wings. This does not necessarily follow, however. Gabriel's flight here did not depend on wings for locomotion, and the angels Isaiah saw were only in vision.

In verse 22 Gabriel told Daniel that he had come to give him "skill and understanding" in respect to what Daniel had just petitioned. In fact, he said that at the beginning of Daniel's prayer the commandment was issued for him to come, because God greatly loved Daniel. In view of such divine favor, then, Daniel should give close attention to what Gabriel would say. What a high honor it was for Daniel to be told by an angel that he was "greatly beloved" of God.

2. *The seventy weeks outlined in general (Dan. 9:24)*

In verse 24 Gabriel spoke specifically of the seventy weeks. He did so first in general terms, citing six matters that would be accomplished in respect to Israel during this time period. As noted earlier, these "weeks" are not periods of seven days each, but seven years each. The Hebrew word means simply "sevens." The thought could be "sevens" of days or "sevens" of years. The context indicates that the latter is the meaning here. In fact, the Israelites were quite familiar with the idea of sevens of years as well as sevens of days. Their sabbatical year was built on this basis (one year in seven having to be set aside for resting the land, Lev. 25; Deut. 15). Furthermore, the seventy-year period of captivity was based on the idea that seventy of these sabbatical years had not been kept (see 2 Chron. 36:21; cf. Lev. 26:33-35; Jer. 34:12-22). Knowing this, Daniel would have recognized that the seventy years of the captivity represented seventy sevens of years in which these violations had occurred; he would have understood Gabriel to be saying simply that another period, similar in length to that which had made the captivity necessary, was coming in the future experience of the people.

Gabriel here spoke of six things that would be accomplished during these 490 total years. The first four all pertain to making people righteous in the sight of God. The first is "to finish [better, "restrain"] the transgression"; the second, "to make an end of sins"; the third, "to make reconciliation for iniquity"; and the fourth, "to bring in everlasting righteousness." The first three things concern doing away with sin, the first two of these speaking generally, and the third referring to the method, namely, reconciliation or atonement. Such atonement for the riddance of sin was provided by Christ at His first coming. The fourth matter speaks of the result of Christ's atonement in putting away sin: righteousness is applied to lives. In place of unwanted sin, then, righteousness can come in.

All these matters pertain in the first place to Christ's first coming. Gabriel thus was saying that during the projected seventy "weeks," Christ would make atonement for sin (which had been the cause of the Jewish captivity), so that this terrible sin could be replaced by righteousness. These matters pertain in a secondary sense also to the general time of Christ's second coming. This follows from the fact that these words were directed primarily to the Jewish people (see v. 24), and the time when they as a people will avail themselves of this righteousness will be only at that second coming (see Jer. 31:33; Ezek. 37:23; Zech. 13:1; Rom. 11:25-27).

The last two things that will occur during the seventy "weeks" pertain almost exclusively to the second-coming time. The first of these is "to seal up the vision and prophecy." Only by the events of the last days will all "vision and prophecy" be sealed up (fulfilled). Then the last is "to anoint the most Holy" (literally, "holy of holies"). This phrase, "holy of holies," is used thirty-nine times in the Old Testament, always in reference to the Tabernacle or Temple or to the holy articles used in them. It should certainly be understood in the same way here, then, and not as a reference to Christ (as held by some who follow an amillennial interpretation of the passage). Christ's millennial rule will know a restored Temple (see Isa. 66:20, 21; Jer. 33:15-18; Ezek. 20:40, 41; 37:26, 27; 40-46; Zech. 14:16, 17), and it is logical to see it as the point of reference of the phrase.

In summary, the purpose of the verse is to state three main truths to the Jews of Daniel's day: first, these coming seventy weeks of years would concern two occasions of the Messiah's appearance on earth; second, in the first appearance He would provide for the riddance of sin, which had necessitated their captivity, and replace it with righteousness; and third, in his second appearance there would be a time of full application of this righteousness to the people, as all vision and prophecy would come to complete fulfillment and a new Temple would be anointed for service, where they as righteous people might worship as God desired.

3. *Some details regarding the first sixty-nine weeks (Dan. 9:25, 26)*

Verses 25 and 26 deal with the first sixty-nine weeks of years, indicating that 483 years would elapse between a commandment to rebuild Jerusalem and the appearance of Christ, here called "Messiah the Prince." There were three different times when Persian rulers gave commandment for Jerusalem's restoration: first, 538 B.C., Daniel's own day (Ezra 1:2-4); second, 458 B.C., Ezra's time (Ezra 7:11-26); and third, 445 B.C., Nehemiah's time (Neh. 1:3; 2:3-8). The first cannot be the one here in reference, because more than 483 years transpired after it before Christ was even born. Many expositors favor the third one, 445 B.C., because it provides the most explicit directions of the three commandments to rebuild Jerusalem. Sir Robert Anderson made some remarkable mathematical calculations to fit the idea of 483 years to this date so that they ended exactly (to the day) on what he believed was the day of Christ's triumphal entry into Jerusalem.[1] However, his calculations have been frequently challenged; also, he takes the year of Christ's crucifixion as A.D. 32, rather than A.D. 30, which most New Testament students favor.[2]

In the light of this objection, the second time of commandment, 458 B.C., may be the best. Figuring on the basis of normal years, the 483-year period then ends at A.D. 26 (only one year separates 1 B.C. and A.D. 1), and this is the generally accepted date of Jesus'

[1]He figured from March 14, 445 B.C. (first of Nisan, in Artaxerxes twentieth year, Neh. 2:1) to April 6, A.D. 32 (date of triumphal entry, according to Anderson) and found that 173,880 days separated these two dates, which is exactly 483 years ("prophetic" years of 360 days, cf. Rev. 11:2, 3; 12:6; 13:5). See Anderson, *The Coming Prince*, pp. 51-129; cf. A. J. McClain, *Daniel's Prophecy of the Seventy Weeks*, for a condensed presentation.

[2]For a recent article in defense of the A.D. 32 date, however, see R. E. Showers, *Grace Journal*, 11 (Winter, 1970), pp. 30ff.

baptism and the beginning of His ministry. Some have objected that little was actually said in this second commandment regarding the rebuilding of Jerusalem. In reply, however, it may be stated that both the commandment and Ezra's resultant work did concern rebuilding Jerusalem in a moral and spiritual way, and there is reason to believe that substantial building activities of a physical nature occurred as well (see Ezra 9:9).

The reason for the division of the sixty-nine weeks into seven weeks (49 years) and sixty-two weeks (434 years) seems to be to separate the seven weeks as the time in which the complete rebuilding of Jerusalem was accomplished. The closing words of verse 25 are best taken with this significance: "The street shall be built again, and the wall [or moat]." It is quite possible that Nehemiah lived and worked in this rebuilding effort until the year 409 B.C., which would be just 49 years after 458 B.C.[3]

Verse 26 describes what would happen to the Messiah the Prince after sixty-two more weeks had elapsed (or, after A.D. 26, according to the above reckoning). No indication is given as to how long after, but at least sometime after the close of those weeks He would be "cut off." The reference is certainly to Christ's crucifixion, which would have occurred approximately three-and-a-half years after the end of those weeks, figuring from the time of His baptism. Then another major event is indicated as happening after that close: the destruction of "the city and the sanctuary" (Jerusalem and the Temple). This occurred in A.D. 70, approximately forty years after the crucifixion. It would be effected by "the people of the prince that shall come." History indicates that these people were the Romans, under the leadership of Titus Vespasian. When the Roman army came in response to a revolt by the Jews, the end of both Jerusalem and the Temple was indeed brought about by a "flood" of destruction, and, "unto the end of the war" that was fought, desolate conditions were truly determined on both city and Temple. The reason for mentioning this time of destruction in this context seems to be two-fold: first, to present a full cycle in respect to Jerusalem and the Temple, from their being rebuilt at the beginning of this seventy-week period to their destruction again after the close of sixty-nine of the weeks; second, to prefigure the later destruction of both of them again by the Antichrist, who would appear in the seventieth week, yet to be discussed.

[3]For discussion, see L. J. Wood, *Commentary on Daniel*, p. 254.

4. The seventieth week (Dan. 9:27)

a. Identification of the Antichrist as the central figure. The seventieth week is presented at the beginning of verse 27: "And he shall confirm the covenant [literally, "a covenant," without the definite article] with many for one week." The previous verse presents two possibilities for the antecedent of the pronoun "he": the Messiah who is cut off or the prince who is of the people who would destroy the city and Temple. Several matters favor the latter.

First, this prince is the nearer of the two antecedents grammatically.

Second, the unusual manner of reference in verse 26 to this person calls for just such a further reference as this. There is really no reason for him to be mentioned in that verse, unless he would be further involved in the discussion. Some expositors have taken him to be Titus Vespasian, who did have a part in leading against the city in A.D. 70, but Titus was hardly of sufficient significance to this context to warrant the manner of mention given here.

Third, several matters show that the reference does not fit if it is taken as the Messiah, Christ. (1) This person is said to "confirm [literally, "cause to be strong"] a covenant," but Christ made no covenant. God made a covenant of grace with man and Christ fulfilled requirements under it, but this is quite different from Christ making a covenant. (2) Even if Christ had made a covenant, it would be unusual to mention it here and not before, when the subjects of His death and even the destruction of Jerusalem were set forth in verse 26. (3) The idea of the seventieth week, here associated with this person, does not fit the life or ministry of Christ, as will be shown presently.

Fourth, in contrast, several considerations show that "the prince that shall come" fits very well as the antecedent when he is understood to be the little horn (Antichrist) of chapter 7. (1) He is said to be of the Roman people, which will be true of the Antichrist, as noted in chapter 7 (see under Dan. 7:8, 23, 24). (2) The use of the term "prince" for this one (the exact same Hebrew term used for Christ in verse 25) identifies him as one who will be in some sense parallel with Christ in his role, and this will be uniquely true of the Antichrist, who will be Satan's counterfeit for Christ. (3) The definite article is used with the participle, translated in verse 26, "that shall come" (literally, "the one coming"), indicating that this one would be important and probably was mentioned earlier in the book, as is true of the Antichrist. (4) Since the Antichrist was presented in Daniel's two earlier visions, as has been seen, and again in the fourth, it might be expected that he would be involved in this third one as well. (5) The description of the deeds of this one in the remainder of the verse fits all that is revealed elsewhere regarding activities of the Antichrist, as we will observe later.

b. Matters pertaining to the seventieth week. Now that we have discussed the identity of the antecedent, we can move on to consider the "one week," the seventieth of the total seventy. It is treated separately from the first sixty-nine because it is the one part of the total seventy weeks which deals with the time of Christ's second coming. This event still lies in the future today, which means that the time-gap involved here is the same as the one in Nebuchadnezzar's dream and Daniel's first two visions. Because the Antichrist is active during this seven-year period (cf. discussion under Dan. 2:41-43; 7:8, 23-25; 8:23-25; 11:36-45), the period is to be identified with the great tribulation, desciptions of which appear frequently in Scripture (e.g., Ps. 2:5; Jer. 30:3-11; Ezek. 20:33-44; Matt. 24:15-24; Rev. 6-18).

The objection most often raised to this interpretation is that it posits a time-gap between the sixty-ninth and seventieth weeks. It is argued that if Daniel spoke of a period of seventy weeks, these weeks should be seen to run continuously, without break. Several reasons exist, however, which show the fact of this time-gap.

First, the text itself treats the seventieth week separately from the first sixty-nine, suggesting something unique about it, such as that it occurred only after a gap in time. Second, the text further indicates directly that a time-gap of at least forty-three years existed. This number of years elapsed after the close of the sixty-nine weeks, while the crucifixion and destruction of Jerusalem occurred, both of which are mentioned in verse 26 prior to the reference to the seventieth week in verse 27. This fact alone destroys the basic idea of continuity for all seventy weeks. Third, the idea of fitting this seventieth week into the life of Christ is quite impossible, as noted. Neither His life nor His ministry lasted seven years. Sometimes it is noted that His crucifixion came approximately at the close of the first half of such a period (three-and-a-half years after the baptism, which is correct) and that the last half could refer to the continuation of His ministry from heaven. But, if so, why stop in that continued ministry after only another three-and-a-half years? Nothing is known to have occurred at that time to support this suggestion. Fourth, the idea of a time-gap should not be thought strange, for it has already been seen in chapters 2, 7, and 8 and will be seen again in chapter 11. The rationale for such a gap is simply that there was a need to speak prophetically of both advents of Christ, and there was no need to describe the history between them, particularly since that history would concern Gentiles primarily, and Gabriel's message concerned Jews (v. 24). Fifth, the message of Gabriel already implied a time-gap, because in verse 24 the six matters specified call for both advents of Christ to fulfill them, as noted. Sixth, in Matthew 24:15 (cf. Mark 13:14), Jesus referred to the "abomination of desolation, spoken of by Daniel the prophet," as something yet future to His time, and, as will be shown presently, Jesus was referring to a feature of this seventieth week which is mentioned here in Daniel 9:27.

c. Two main events in this week. Verse 27 presents two main events of this seventieth week. The first is that at its beginning the Antichrist will make a covenant with many. The "many" in reference must be the Jewish people, because the whole message regards them (v. 24). Since the word for "covenant" does not have the article (contrary to the translation in the King James Version), the covenant in view need not be some historic agreement, but one that will be seen as pertinent to that particular time. It will likely be a mutual-recognition, non-aggression type of treaty made between the Antichrist and Israel. Such an agreement makes sense from Israel's point of view (at least in terms of today's history), for Israel, restored as a sovereign nation since 1948, is looking for friends. For a person with the power and stature of the king of restored Rome to desire to make a treaty with them would be most welcome, indeed. It also makes sense from the Antichrist's point of view (again in light of today's world situation),[4] because he, as king of a revived Roman Empire, would logically be opposed to the present Russian-Arab bloc, which is united against Israel, seeing it as a potential threat to his ambitions. Therefore, he would be likely to side with Israel. It may be added that, as long as such a treaty remained in force, Israel would have a much easier time in world affairs than at present, for the weight of the Roman confederacy would be a significant source of strength.

The second main event is that "in the midst of the week" the Antichrist will break this treaty by ordering "the sacrifice and oblation to cease" at what will be a restored Temple by that time. It

---

[4]One must be careful not to be too specific in prophetic prediction, but he also should be aware of "the signs of the times" existent at any point in history.

appears, then, that at the beginning of this week, the Antichrist will make a covenant to last for seven years with Israel, but that halfway through he will find reason to break it. The reason will be seen in the discussion of Daniel 11:40, 41. This means that the first half of the seven-year time will be pleasant for Israel, but the last half will become very unpleasant. In fact, it will be terrible, for the Antichrist will then become as much Israel's enemy as he was its friend during the first half of this period. He will begin to act toward the Jews in the pattern of Antiochus Ephiphanes, as noted in chapter 8.[5] The most likely time for Israel to rebuild the Temple may be during the peaceful years under the Antichrist's protection. At least it will have to have been reconstructed by the midpoint of the tribulation week, for its sacrifices and offerings then to be ordered to cease.

d. Trouble at the hand of the Antichrist. The remainder of verse 27 concerns the trouble and suffering the Antichrist will bring on Israel, after he has broken the covenant. The Hebrew of this last portion of the verse is difficult, but it is probably best translated as follows: ". . . even unto the overspreading of abominations of desolation; and unto the end even what has been determined shall be poured out upon the desolate."

Notice first that the phrase "abominations of desolation" is the same as the one used by Christ in Matthew 24:15 (except that "abominations" is plural here, whereas it is singular there — something of little if any significance). When Christ referred to "the abomination of desolation, spoken of by Daniel the prophet," He must have meant this very phrase in Daniel 9:27. He spoke of this "abomination" as something which would be made to "stand in the holy place" during the great tribulation (cf. Matt. 24:21). Notice also that the same phrase, "abomination of desolation," was used by Daniel later in reference to Antiochus Epiphanes (Dan. 11:31) as something which this man established in the Temple in his day. Since Antiochus was typical of the Antichrist, as has been seen, it follows that what the Antichrist will set up in his day will be in the pattern of what Antiochus did. From 1 Maccabees 1:45-54 we learn that Antiochus, following his order forbidding the Temple ceremonies to be continued (parallel to Daniel 9:27 regarding the Antichrist), "set up the abomination of desolation upon the altar" and built "altars throughout the cities of Judah on every side." Then,

[5]See chap. 8, pp. 103, 104.

2 Maccabees 6:2 indicates that in this way he polluted "the temple in Jerusalem and [called] it the temple of Jupiter Olympius." The exact identity of this "abomination of desolation" he set up is not made clear in these passages, but it almost certainly was either an altar to Jupiter Olympius or else an actual statue to this Grecian god, or possibly both.

It follows, then, that the Antichrist, shortly after his order at the midpoint of the tribulation week that sacrifice and offering cease, will set up in the restored Temple something detestable, like a false altar or a great statue (possibly of himself), which will cause a desolating condition there (as Antiochus' action did in his day). Jewish worshipers will refuse to come to the Temple under such conditions.

The remainder of the verse indicates that until the end of the remaining three-and-a-half years of the seventieth week, all that has been predetermined in respect to suffering will be poured out upon the desolate city of Jerusalem and the Temple. Because of the parallel with Antiochus Epiphanes, it is clear that what will be "poured out" will be terrible in its effect on the Jews. According to Zechariah 13:8, 9, no less than two-thirds of Israel's population will be slaughtered during this time — a degree of death in terms of a nation's total population that this world has never seen. It is no wonder that Jeremiah spoke of it as "the time of Jacob's trouble" (Jer. 30:7). It is in this connection that the reference to the Jerusalem destruction of A.D. 70 (v. 26), when so many Jews were killed by the Romans, becomes helpful.

For Further Study

1. Read articles in a Bible dictionary or encyclopedia on: (a) Artaxerxes Longimanus, (b) Gabriel, (c) abomination of desolation.
2. How did Daniel know that the captivity would last seventy years?
3. What was Daniel's main request in his prayer?
4. On what did he lay stress in his prayer, however? Why?
5. Give in years the length of each of the divisions of the total seventy-week period predicted by Gabriel.
6. What two events are said to occur after the first sixty-nine weeks?
7. Give evidences that a long time-gap exists between the sixty-ninth and the seventieth weeks.
8. What will happen at the beginning of the seventieth week? At its midpoint?
9. Contrast conditions for the Jews during the first half of this week and the second half.

Chapter 10

The Fourth Vision: Supernatural Powers in Conflict

The fourth and last of Daniel's predictive revelations is now presented. Differing from the first three visions, this one is recorded over three chapters, the last three of the book. This occasion of revelation deals with approximately the same periods of history as set forth in the vision of chapter 8 (the periods of Medo-Persia, Greece, and the great tribulation). Considerably more detail is given, however, especially concerning events after Alexander the Great and during the time of the great tribulation. The information is presented through a heavenly messenger, much as in chapter 9, and not by means of symbolism as in the first two visions.

The present chapter tells of the coming of this heavenly messenger for the purpose of imparting the information to Daniel. The account of his coming is significant, because it involves his conflict with an emissary of Satan. It either states directly or implies several important facts about angels and demons and their respective interests in the people and work of God.

A. The General Setting (Dan. 10:1-3)

1. *Introductory matters (Dan. 10:1)*

For the fourth time, Daniel began by indicating the date of the revelation concerned. It is quite evident that he believed the chronological relation of these occasions to each other, and to other events, was significant. This present occasion came in the third year of Cyrus, which means just two years after Gabriel's appearance to Daniel in chapter 9. (Darius and Cyrus were contemporary rulers, so their first years of reign were the same.) The four occasions of revelation came in groups of two, then: in the first and third years of Belshazzar and the first and third years of Cyrus (Darius), with thirteen years intervening. At the time of this fourth instance, Daniel was about eighty-four years of age.

One significant matter to note is that this fourth occasion of revelation followed the return of the Jews to Judah by about two years. Daniel had prayed in Cyrus' first year (Dan. 9:1) that this return might soon be permitted, and God answered that prayer affirmatively. It was in that same year (the first year of Cyrus) that Cyrus issued the remarkable decree that made it possible (2 Chron. 36:22; Ezra 1:1). The actual return may have been effected that year or at least no later than the next (538/537 B.C.). Since Daniel was still in Babylon in this third year of Cyrus, it is evident that he did not accompany the group, perhaps for two reasons: his advanced age and his high position in the government as one of Darius' three presidents, where he could wield so much influence for good on behalf of his fellow people.

Another significant matter relates to Daniel's experience in the lions' den. This, too, occurred in Darius' early years, as we noted. Since there is no way to know the time exactly, it is impossible to say whether it occurred before or after this fourth time of revelation, but it probably was about the same time.

The closing words of verse 1 indicate that Daniel was able to understand this revelation when given. In fact, that the thought is repeated may intend to say that, because of this final revelation, Daniel was able to understand more fully what had been set forth also in the first three.

2. Daniel's personal preparation (Dan. 10:2, 3)

This occasion of revelation differed from the others in that it came at the close of three weeks of spiritual preparation by Daniel. Verse 2 says that Daniel had been "mourning" for three weeks; according to verse 3, that meant he had been fasting, for one thing. The purpose of this mourning, according to verse 12, was that Daniel might "understand"; the context set forth by both verses 1 and 12 show that the understanding he sought pertained to Israel's future. He wanted the best for his own people and wondered how God would work this out. One cannot conclude from this that Daniel thought his mourning in this way would necessarily lead to another occasion of revelation, but the fact that God did see fit to bring the revelation at this time suggests that the demonstration of a proper attitude of heart is conducive to receiving revelation (cf. 2 Kings 3:15).

Holding the high position he did, Daniel must have been busy; that he took three weeks for this time of spiritual discipline is noteworthy. It shows that he placed a high priority on his own spiritual standing in the sight of God. To Daniel, his personal relationship with God was more important than earthly concerns.

Not only do we know that these three weeks occurred in the first year of Cyrus' reign, but from verse 4 we learn that the twenty-fourth day of the first month (Nisan) brought them to a close. They had begun, then, on the third of the month. During these three weeks, Daniel did not eat "pleasant" (delectable) food, nor any meat, nor did he drink any wine. This does not necessarily mean that he ate no food at all, but that he abstained from fine food, which was readily available to him as Darius' high officer. Also, he refrained from anointing himself. It was a custom to anoint oneself daily with oil to avoid being burned by the hot sun. Anointing was a sign of joy (Prov. 27:9), and it was normally discontinued in this way during times of mourning (cf. 2 Sam. 12:20; 14:2).

B. The Appearance of the Heavenly Messenger (Dan. 10:4-8)

1. *Description of the messenger (Dan. 10:4-6)*

As Daniel came to speak of the appearance of a glorious visitor from heaven, he first told a little more as to his situation at the time. For one thing, he stated that the exact day was the twenty-fourth of this month, as just noted. This means that the important day of Passover (the fourteenth of Nisan) had just passed, as well as the Feast of Unleavened Bread (fifteenth to twenty-first; Exod. 12:14-18). In fact, it is probable that this special time of the year had prompted Daniel to use these three weeks for this occasion of mourning. Then Daniel located himself at the time of the appearance: he was standing beside the Hiddekel (Tigris) River. This means that he was not in Babylon, for it is the Euphrates River that flowed through that city. The Tigris is located a few miles to the east. It may be noted, also, that he was there in actuality, and not merely in vision (as was true regarding the Ulai River in chapter 9), for he had attendants with him.

It was on this day, then, and in this place that Daniel saw the grand person described. The identity of this person is difficult to determine. He may have been Gabriel; but it is strange, then, that he was not named as he was in the previous two times of revelation (8:16; 9:21). Also, one must ask why he should be described here in this third appearance rather than in the first. This may have been the second person of the Godhead, here in theophany, since the description given is much like that of Christ in John's vision on Patmos years later (Rev. 1:13-16). A difficulty arises, however, because this one spoke of receiving assistance from the chief angel Michael in a conflict with one called "the prince of the kingdom of Persia" (v. 13). It is not likely that a mere angel could be — or would be called upon to be—of assistance to Christ. This cannot have been Michael either, for this one is said to receive help from Michael, as we just noted. The most likely identity is that this one was simply another angel, perhaps of parallel importance with Gabriel and Michael, whose name, for some reason, is not recorded.

In Daniel's description of this person, he first noted his clothing. It was made of linen (thus it was white, speaking of purity), with a gold girdle, that is, a sash two to six inches wide, worn about the waist. Then Daniel described the person's body, insofar as it was visible. He said his skin looked like "beryl" (Tarshish stone), which has a yellow and gold luster and is quartzlike in structure (cf. Ezek. 1:16; 10:9). His face seemed like "lightning," probably meaning that it shone with brilliance; in the midst of this brilliance glowed the person's eyes, shining still more brightly — like "lamps of fire." Daniel further described the exposed arms and feet as looking like "polished brass." As the person began to speak, Daniel heard his words as though from a vast crowd speaking in unison: strong, deep, and authoritative. The person was human in form, then, but awesome to look at. The intention no doubt was to impress Daniel with this person's heavenly origin and to assure him that his word, therefore, would be accurate and reliable.

2. *Reaction of Daniel and his attendants (Dan. 10:7, 8)*

Daniel alone saw this person, and not the attendants that were with him. This of itself would suggest that the appearance was in vision only, not in actual corporeal form. In verses 10 and 16, however, this person is said to touch Daniel for the purpose of strengthening him, and this indicates a real appearance. Perhaps the best explanation is that God somehow "clouded" the vision of these companions, so that the heavenly visitor was made invisible to them.[1] They were probably pagans, and God may have seen them as unfit subjects to view so glorious a representative from heaven. That "a

[1]A parallel situation occurred years later when Saul of Tarsus was on his way to Damascus with companions (Acts 9:3-7).

great quaking" (trembling) came on them at the time Daniel saw this man shows they were aware he did see someone unusual; they reacted by becoming fearful and fleeing in panic from the place.

When these assistants fled, Daniel was left alone; this was good and probably planned by God. Daniel could concentrate better now on what was said by his visitor. Daniel's first reaction was also one of fear, resulting in a loss of strength. His facial expression changed from his normal "comeliness" to one of "corruption." The meaning is that a deathlike paleness came on him, probably with a grotesque wrenching of features, giving a picture of one horror stricken.

C. Explanatory Words of the Heavenly Messenger (Dan. 10:9-14)

The next verses tell that the heavenly messenger imparted strength to Daniel and then stated the reason for not having come to Daniel sooner. He said that he had been hindered on the way by one identified as "the prince of the kingdom of Persia."

1. *Restrengthening of Daniel (Dan. 10:9-11)*

Daniel's first need, as the messenger was about to speak to him, was to regain sufficient emotional strength to comprehend what was to be said. It appears that Daniel, on first seeing the glorious person, fell prostrate in a "deep sleep" (fainting spell). Consequently, a hand was extended to touch him (no doubt by the messenger), with the result that he was able to rise to a "hands-and-knees" position (v. 10). The messenger continued to encourage him by speaking of him as "greatly beloved" (the same phrase as in Dan. 9:23), thus seeking to give him reassurance in this awesome occasion (v. 11). The messenger further told him to stand fully upright and understand the words about to be spoken. Then Daniel did arise, though he was still trembling. We should remember that Daniel was in no way an immature person in all this. He was about eighty-four years old, a truly spiritually mature person who had already experienced three moving revelations from God. Therefore, his reaction in this instance shows that the occasion was indeed unusual and that the glory of this heavenly visitor was most overpowering.

2. *A supernatural conflict described (Dan. 10:12-14)*

Finally, the grand visitor was able to begin his message to Daniel. The message itself, regarding information of the future, was imparted later (recorded in chaps. 11 and 12), but the visitor first wanted to let

Daniel know about a supernatural conflict that had just been waged. The conflict had been fought so that he might now be with Daniel to reveal that information. The messenger stated that actually he had left — apparently, God's presence — to come to Daniel on the first day of Daniel's mourning, meaning three weeks before. Already at that time, he said, God had heard Daniel's petition and commissioned a reply to be communicated. The fact that the messenger spoke of Daniel's words having been heard indicates that Daniel had been praying during these three weeks as well as mourning and fasting. This was not said before but was surely to be expected.

Verse 13 tells why the visitor had arrived three weeks later. He had been "withstood" by "the prince of the kingdom of Persia," and had found it necessary to wage this conflict with him. He had been able to achieve victory, however, and to come on to where Daniel was. He further stated that he had been aided in this victory by Michael, who had come to help him (v. 13).

Before considering the identification of this hindering prince, it is well to observe that God was gracious toward Daniel in thus responding to his prayer. He saw fit not only to give him an answer as he sought to know Israel's future but to give it through the medium of a personal heavenly messenger. He might have used a dream or a vision, but He chose this more intimate method. Surely Daniel was highly honored by God in this.

The one who had hindered God's special messenger can only have been a demon, appointed to do this by the chief of demons, Satan himself. This follows from the fact that he sought to hinder an order of God from being carried out, and he was certainly more than human to be able to war against such a supernatural messenger, commissioned by God. That he is called "the prince of the kingdom of Persia" must mean that he had been assigned by Satan to effect Satan's program in connection with the Persian government. His assignment to that end was evidently a continuing one, for later (v. 20) Daniel's visitor said he would personally return to do further battle with him. The nature of this demon's assignment may be conjectured as being to hinder God's will in whatever way Persia was concerned. More particularly, it would have involved God's people there, prompting the Persian king to show ill will and disfavor toward them, refusing requests they might bring, and imposing hardship in general. Then, it is noteworthy that the messenger spoke later (v. 20) of a prince of Greece eventually being assigned. Since God's people would be under Greek rule following Alexander's defeat of Medo-Persia, it is logical to believe that this assignment would be made at that time and that the purpose would be the same, namely to hinder God's work and program with His people during the supremacy of Greece.

These thoughts lead to the conclusion that Satan is interested in hindering God's work with His people at any time and that he may assign special emissaries to influence governments at the highest level to hinder that work. Certainly this chapter carries significance regarding the nature of struggles between higher powers in reference to God's program on earth (cf. Eph. 6:11, 12).

"Michael, one of the chief princes" aided Daniel's visitor. Michael is mentioned three times in the Old Testament — all three instances being in the book of Daniel (10:13, 21; 12:1) — and twice in the New Testament (Jude 9; Rev. 12:7). That he is called here "one of the chief princes" agrees with Jude's description of him as "archangel." He appears to have been the highest of the angels. According to Daniel 10:21 and 12:1, Michael was assigned by God particularly as Israel's prince. That God should choose the chief angel for this task surely signifies the greatness of God's interest in His chosen people. Michael came to the assistance of Daniel's visitor, and between the two of them victory was achieved over Satan's representative. It is impossible for mortal man to imagine the character of such a supernatural conflict. But that it was real is emphasized by the fact that it lasted three weeks.

That Daniel's visitor is said to have "remained there with the kings of Persia" is best taken to mean that he remained preeminent (as on a field of battle, standing victorious), having won this struggle, and therefore he had the desired influence over the kings of Persia. In other words, because of the victory by God's messenger, Satan at the moment did not have the influence he wanted in the Persian government, but God did, through this angel. This suggests that the conflict waged had been basically over this position of influence. Satan's emissary had held it, thus working to the detriment of God's program and people; but God's angel had come and fought him for it, no doubt as a part of his assigned mission in coming to Daniel, and had defeated him. After the conflict had been won, while still holding this important place of influence, the messenger had come on to deliver the message to Daniel.

In verse 14, the messenger stated that he had arrived for the purpose of helping Daniel understand what would occur in the "latter days" of his people. "Latter days" is the same expression as used in Daniel 2:28 (q.v.), and the time in mind is indicated by the ensuing message in chapters 11 and 12; namely, days yet future with stress on the times of Antiochus Epiphanes and the great tribulation. Note that the weight of the messenger's words concerned what would happen to Daniel's people, the Jews, rather than the Gentiles. The force of the closing words, "the vision is for many days," is that the prediction about to be given would concern days far in the future. In the previous three weeks of fasting and prayer, Daniel had no doubt been wondering about the near future of Israel, but the messenger was hereby saying that his information was to concern days in the far future.

D. Daniel Strengthened to Understand (Dan. 10:15 – 11:1)

At these initial words, Daniel was again overcome with emotion. The messenger ceased to speak while he ministered to Daniel's need once more. Then the angel went on with words of explanation, building on what he had thus far said.

1. *Further strengthening of Daniel (Dan. 10:15-19)*

Daniel now turned his face to the ground and remained speechless. He actually had not spoken to the visitor even once, and he now continued to be silent as he again became weak. Seeing the return of this deep emotional upheaval, the messenger ceased talking and put forth his hand to touch Daniel's lips. The effect was to start Daniel speaking for the first. It may be that he had been emotionally incapable of speech before. The words Daniel uttered were that sorrow had come on him because of the vision, so that no strength remained within him. In other words, he again felt as he had a moment before — incapable of comprehending what the messenger was saying. Then he continued by giving an explanation of his feelings. How could he, being merely a servant, possibly speak with his "lord" in this face-to-face manner? At this, the messenger once more came near enough to touch Daniel and impart the strength he needed. He accompanied the touch by telling Daniel again that he was "greatly beloved," no doubt with the same purpose in mind as the first time. Then Daniel, feeling the new surge of strength, bid the messenger to continue speaking.

2. *The continued message (Dan. 10:20 – 11:1)*

The messenger continued. He began with the use of a rhetorical question: "Do you know why I have come to you?" His intention was to impress Daniel with the truth that the messenger's coming had been for a larger reason than what seemed obvious. Before the break in the earlier words, the messenger had stated this obvious reason: that his coming had been to give Daniel information in response to his prayer. He had also included an indication of the larger reason, namely, that a major conflict was being waged among supernatural powers concerning Israel's welfare. Now he would continue speaking about this warfare, and he wanted Daniel to know that this warfare was truly involved in the full reason for his coming.

Thus he continued by saying that he was about to return to take up again the "fight with the prince of Persia." This Satan-assigned demon had not given up in the conflict, then, but would be waiting to fight again over the position of influence in Persia when Daniel's visitor returned to the place of battle. The visitor added that when he had "gone forth" from having won over this prince of Persia, a prince of Greece would become the next enemy to encounter in a similar manner. As noted earlier, this new prince would doubtless be a demon assigned to hinder God's program with His people when they came under the jurisdiction of Greece. Because this time would not be for another two centuries (Persian history continued from this present moment of c. 536 B.C. to Alexander's conquest in 331 B.C.), the thought is that the messenger would be continuing to fight with the Persian demon for that length of time before having to begin with the Grecian one.

Again it is appropriate to comment that such words are most significant regarding the conflict of supernatural powers in respect to God's program and people. The implication is clear that Satan works at the highest levels to oppose what God desires to see accomplished. He had apparently assigned a demon to concentrate on influencing the Persian kings to work to Israel's detriment, as long as Persia was in control over God's people; when the control changed to Greece, he would assign one to concentrate similarly there. Significantly, however, God's representative would be on hand to oppose both, first in Persia as long as the Persian demon was active and then in Greece when the Grecian demon came on the scene.

In verse 21, the messenger reassured Daniel that before returning to carry on this conflict he would communicate to him "that which is noted in the scripture of truth." The phrase "scripture of truth" simply means, "that which God had declared concerning the future events here in view."

Also in verse 21, the messenger stated that he alone would be active in contending with Satan's assigned demons in the manner just indicated, but that Michael, Israel's prince, would be available to give help at any time (as he had in the immediately preceding days). As has been observed, Michael's main task was to oversee matters pertaining especially to the Jews; but since Jewish welfare was vitally involved with the dominating empire of the day, it fell to him to assist in that respect as well whenever the need might arise.

The first verse of chapter 11 belongs with chapter 10, giving a concluding note to it. In it the messenger added the historic note that a previous time had existed when it had been necessary for him to come to Michael's aid (implying that their help was mutual and not just one-sided). The time had been in Darius' first year, which would have been the general time of the Jews' return to Judah under Sheshbazzar (see Ezra 1:1-11). Michael, wanting this return to be effected, may have encountered difficulty in influencing Darius and Cyrus to that end, and Daniel's visitor could have helped bring the influence. At least they had worked together to accomplish the desire of God. The general truth of the chapter is that great battles take place among the higher powers in respect to God's program and people here on earth. How dependent God's people are that God's angels faithfully wage this warfare on their behalf.

For Further Study

1. Read articles in a Bible dictionary or encyclopedia on: (a) angels, (b) demons, (c) Michael.
2. Indicate the probable identification of the heavenly messenger and describe him.
3. With whom did he have to contend before reaching Daniel?
4. What was the issue in this conflict?
5. What significance do you see in the fact that Daniel became weak in the presence of this messenger?
6. What two beings would the messenger have to fight after leaving Daniel?
7. What outstanding truth can be drawn from this chapter?

Chapter 11

The Fourth Vision: The Vision Proper

With this chapter the predictive portion of Daniel's fourth revelation begins. The heavenly messenger had finished with his preliminary words to Daniel, and he was ready to take up the message that he had come especially to deliver.

The stress of this predictive portion is on Antiochus Epiphanes (vv. 21-35) and then on the Antichrist (vv. 36-45), the former typifying the latter, as has been seen. Again, an implied time-gap exists between the two. Both are identified not by name but only by a description of their characters and actions, which has been found true also in the previous contexts considered. Before mentioning either of the two main characters, however, the messenger tells of history preceding Antiochus. First, early Persian rulers are mentioned; then Alexander the Great, who defeated Persia. After this comes a remarkably detailed description of successive kings who ruled two of the divisions of Alexander's empire: the Egyptian division under the Ptolemies (descendants of the first ruler of this division, Ptolemy), and the Syrian division under the Seleucids (descendants of the first ruler of this division, Seleucus). These two divisions call for this manner of attention because the affairs of Palestine, which lay precisely between the two, were so often involved in their mutual conflicts. Palestine came under the control first of the southern division and then of the northern. Warfare raged over its territory again and again, as the two divisions fought each other. The detail of history presented in this portion provides one of the most remarkable predictive sections of all Scripture.

A. History Until the Division of Alexander's Empire (Dan. 11:2-4)

The messenger began his predictive message by telling of the period when Daniel yet lived. He spent little time on this, however,

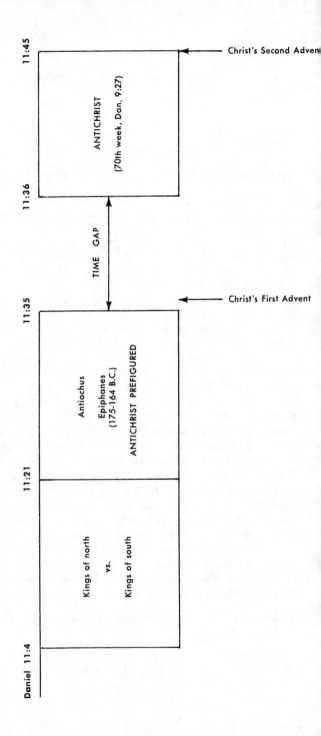

FOURTH VISION

Daniel 11:4

11:21 — Kings of north vs. Kings of south

Antiochus Epiphanes (175-164 B.C.) — ANTICHRIST PREFIGURED

11:35 ← Christ's First Advent

TIME GAP

11:36 — ANTICHRIST (70th week, Dan. 9:27)

11:45 ← Christ's Second Advent

speaking only briefly about either the Medo-Persian period or the meteoric rise of Alexander, a combined span of more than two centuries (539-323 B.C.). He moved on quickly to speak more of the era when Alexander's vast holdings were divided into four parts.

The principal reason for speaking about Persian kings at all was to tell of a fourth one (Xerxes), who would make war on Greece and so give Greece, under Alexander, a reason to retaliate against Persia. Speaking of this fourth king, Daniel's visitor said that there would be three Persian rulers who would precede him. These three are known from secular history, though not named in the text: Cyrus (539-529 B.C.), Cambyses (529-522 B.C.), and Darius Hystaspes (521-486 B.C.). Actually a fourth, named Smerdis, ruled between the last two for about six months, but he clearly was an imposter and was put off the throne with dispatch by Darius Hystaspes; he is rightly omitted from this list, then, by the messenger. It should be mentioned, also, that following Xerxes several other Persian kings ruled before the retaliation of Alexander, but they did nothing more to provoke his anger and therefore are passed over as not significant for mentioning in this context. Their names are: Artaxerxes Longimanus (465-424 B.C.), Xerxes II (424-423 B.C.), Darius II Nothus (423-404 B.C.), Artaxerxes II Mnemom (404-359 B.C.), Artaxerxes III Ochus (359-338 B.C.), Arses (338-336 B.C.), and Darius III Codomannus (336-331 B.C.).

The most significant king here is the fourth one, Xerxes (486-465 B.C.), who made an important expedition against Greece. His father, Darius Hystaspes, had attacked Greece in 490 B.C. but not with the same scope of activity. Xerxes was rich, as indicated. His predecessors had amassed great wealth and he added to it, especially in preparation for the Grecian campaign. His feast of no fewer than 180 days, as described in Esther 1:1-12,[1] depicts something of the grandeur of this preparation. History testifies that he attacked Greece with an enormous army and navy, but was unsuccessful in attempting to avenge the humiliating defeat suffered by his father.

The "mighty king" of verse 3 is the retaliating ruler of Greece, Alexander the Great (336-323 B.C.). He was indeed "mighty" and did "rule with great dominion," as shown especially under Daniel 8:5-8.

Verse 4 speaks again (as in Daniel 8) about his kingdom being

---

[1]The Ahasuerus of Esther is the same as this Xerxes, the name Ahasuerus being a Hebrew equivalent for his Persian name, Khshayarsha. Also, the character of Xerxes fits the biblical picture of Ahasuerus.

"broken" and "divided" into four parts. It is also noted that this division would not be to "his posterity." Alexander's four generals received the empire rather than anyone from his own family.[2] The same verse says further that none of these later rulers maintained the same "dominion" or authority that he wielded; this also came true.

B. The Ptolemies and Seleucids Until Antiochus Epiphanes (Dan. 11:5-20)

Having predicted that there would be four divisions to Alexander's empire, the messenger continued to speak of only two: the Syrian division, just north of Palestine, and the Egyptian division, just south.

1. History until Antiochus the Great (Dan. 11:5-9)

The "king of the south" of verse 5, who would be strong and have a prince that would become yet stronger, was Ptolemy Soter (304-283 B.C.), the general who received the Egyptian division. The prince who became stronger was Seleucus Nicator (304-281 B.C.), the general who received the Syrian division. He is called here the prince of Ptolemy because for a time he was subordinate to Ptolemy, but he broke away to become ruler of the largest of the divisions. As indicated, these two rulers began the two ruling lines, the Ptolemies and the Seleucids.

Verse 6 speaks of a "king's daughter of the south" who made an agreement with the king of the north but did not retain her power. This daughter was Berenice, daughter of Ptolemy Philadelphus (283-246 B.C.), son of Ptolemy Soter. The agreement was for her to marry Antiochus Theos (262-246 B.C.), a grandson of Seleucus Nicator, intending thus to unite the two divisions. However, Berenice and her attendants were all murdered in Syria about three years after the marriage, thus ending this attempt at union and losing for Berenice the power she had planned to achieve. Antiochus Theos, whom she married (the "he" of the phrase, "neither shall he stand") was also murdered by a jealous former wife, who then placed on the Syrian throne her own son, Seleucus Callinicus (246-227 B.C.).

Verses 7-9 tell of a branch of Berenice's roots who came with an army and defeated Seleucus Callinicus. This "branch" was Berenice's brother, Ptolemy Euergetes (246-221 B.C.), who marched north from

---

[2]His own family consisted only of a mentally deficient brother and two infant sons. All three were killed in the ensuing struggle between the generals.

Egypt and attacked Syria, severely defeating Seleucus Callinicus and taking the life of the jealous mother. As verse 8 indicates, he carried booty away to Egypt in great quantity, and he outlived the Syrian ruler by six years.[3] In retaliation, as verse 9 states,[4] Seleucus Callinicus, having regathered his forces, attempted an attack against Egypt (in 240 B.C.) but was unsuccessful and had to return "into his own land" (v. 9).

2. *History of Antiochus the Great (Dan. 11:10-20)*

The two sons of Seleucus Callinicus now enter the picture. They were Seleucus Ceraunus (227-223 B.C.) and Antiochus the Great (223-187 B.C.). Both sons are said to have assembled "great forces," which they did, but before these could be used against Egypt, the older, Seleucus Ceraunus, was killed on a mission in Asia Minor. This left the younger, Antiochus the Great, to pursue matters with Egypt, in accordance with the indication, "one shall certainly come, and overflow, and pass through" (v. 10). This language speaks of victory on his part; he achieved this as he drove the Egyptians back from their position at the north of Palestine, so that he was able to move down into Palestine proper (in 219 B.C.). Then, as the last part of verse 10 indicates, he made a second campaign and this time pushed as far south as Raphia, in southern Palestine, which is probably the "fortress" mentioned here.

The king of the south, who is now said to move in retaliation against Antiochus the Great, was Ptolemy Philopator (221-204 B.C.), son of Ptolemy Euergetes. He was the one just defeated by Antiochus but he retaliated with great strength, the battle being fought at Raphia, the "fortress." The armies of both sides were immense and the battle fierce. This time Ptolemy won. The Hebrew text is not clear, but history shows that "the multitude" that was given into the other's hand was the army of Syria under Antiochus. The text says that, as a result, Ptolemy would be made proud, and this is in keeping with his character; he was a disliked, haughty, profligate person. He was able to inflict terrible slaughter on the Syrian forces, as indicated, but he was not "strengthened" himself. Instead of following

---

[3]Another translation of v. 8 shows the meaning as "standing against" the king of the north rather than "outliving him." This meaning is also satisfied by history, for Ptolemy Euergetes did "stand against" Seleucus Callinicus successfully in a later counterattack brought against him.

[4]A more literal translation of v. 9 than that found in the KJV is, "And one shall come against the kingdom of the king of the south, but he shall return to his own land."

up his victory by pursuing the enemy, he withdrew to his own palace and the life of luxury he loved. This resulted in dissatisfaction on the part of his people and actually made him a weaker ruler than before the victory, strange as that seems.

Verse 13 indicates that "after certain years" Antiochus would return against Egypt with another great army. This he did, after fourteen intervening years, when Ptolemy Epiphanes (203-181 B.C.), the four-year-old son of his former enemy, had just been made king. Verse 14 indicates that Antiochus had help at this time by certain "robbers of thy [Daniel's] people" (meaning apostate Jews who had agreed to aid this pagan); with their help he met and defeated the Egyptian force twice in northern Palestine (v. 15). The second time, he defeated the famed Egyptian general, Scopas, first at Paneas (present Banias) and then at Sidon on the Mediterranean. The result was that now the "glorious land" (Palestine, cf. Dan. 8:9) came under Syrian control and continued so.

Verse 17 refers to Antiochus' attempt at this point to take over Egypt as well, with "the strength of his whole kingdom" behind him. The indication is that he would try this by using one called "the daughter of women." What happened was that Antiochus, rather than invading Egypt with an army, sought to gain this control by marrying his daughter Cleopatra (not the famous Cleopatra of later time) to the young Ptolemy Epiphanes. An agreement to this end was made in 197 B.C. and the marriage took place in 193 B.C.; the delay was because Ptolemy was only ten years old in 197 B.C. The phrase "corrupting her" is better translated "to destroy it," meaning Egypt. That is, Antiochus' purpose in this marriage was to destroy Egypt, expecting that his daughter would cooperate with him in this. As the remainder of the verse indicates, however, she did not cooperate with her father and the plan failed. Instead, she served as a good wife to her husband, not helping Antiochus in his nefarious scheme.

Verse 18 refers to Antiochus' endeavor of 197 B.C. (when he still thought his plan regarding Egypt would work) to extend his influence to the isles of the Aegean by taking Greece. At first he was successful, but then Rome entered the conflict and sent the famous Lucius Scipio Asiaticus against him. Antiochus was defeated and had to give Rome even a part of his own Asiatic territory, thus bringing reproach on himself, as the verse indicates. Verse 19 tells of Antiochus' humble return home and his later death. Little is known of him after this return, perhaps because he died one year later, in 187

B.C. His grand plans had utterly failed, both in Egypt and the Aegean area.

The person described in verse 20 is Antiochus' son, Seleucus Philopator (187-176 B.C.). The kingdom he received from his father was still quite large but bankrupt (a large debt being owed to the Romans). Therefore, he sent a "raiser of taxes" in the "glory of his kingdom" (Palestine). He probably sent collectors to other countries, too, but the one he sent to Palestine is known to have been his prime minister, Heliodorus. This man was sent to seize the rich funds of the Temple treasury in Jerusalem (2 Maccabees 3). The verse continues by saying that Seleucus would "be destroyed, neither in anger, nor in battle"; his death almost certainly came by assassination at the hands of this Heliodorus.

With the indication of this king's death, the preliminary history of the chapter is brought to a close. As noted, it is one of the most detailed predictive portions in all Scripture, and history shows that every detail was carried out just as set forth. It is no wonder that liberal writers hold that it had to be written after the history had occurred. It wasn't, however. It was given by supernatural revelation to Daniel by the glorious messenger from heaven.

C. Antiochus Epiphanes (Dan. 11:21-35)

One of the two main persons of this fourth vision now comes to be described: Antiochus Epiphanes, the Old Testament figure of the Antichrist. He was the son of Antiochus the Great and brother of the last king before him, Seleucus Philopator. The reason for his description at length now is that he did prefigure the Antichrist; this fact should be kept continually in mind as the verses before us are considered.

1. *His rise to power (Dan. 11:21-24)*

The man is first introduced most significantly as "a vile person." He was known to be an untrustworthy schemer. He gave himself the name "Epiphanes," meaning "illustrious," but others often called him "Epimanes," meaning "madman." The indication that the honor of the kingdom had not been given him means that he had seized it, for it was not rightfully his. It belonged to Demetrius Soter, the son of his brother, as observed in chapter 8, but Demetrius was being held hostage at the time in Rome, and Antiochus Epiphanes was quick to take the opportunity to move in himself. He did this, not by war, but "peacefully," using "flatteries" and deceit. He knew the right people to influence, and he flattered them into aiding his cause.

Verses 22 to 24 give a general appraisal of the man's activities. The groups that would be "overflown from before" Antiochus are the armies he encountered, including the army of Egypt; Antiochus proved remarkably successful in his military pursuits. "The prince of the covenant" is probably the Jewish high priest of the day, Onias III. Onias had a brother, Joshua, who was sympathetic to the Grecian ideas of Antiochus, and he received Antiochus' support for deposing Onias and taking the position himself. He then took the Grecian name Jason. Jason, in turn, was replaced by another brother, Menelaus, who continued the pro-Grecian policy, cooperating with Antiochus. In his desire to please Antiochus, Menelaus actually killed the good Onias in Antiochus' fourth year (171 B.C.). Verse 23 describes further Antiochus' deceitful tactics in trying to further his cause: he would break treaties almost as soon as he had made them. For several years, he would "come up" (rise in power) in the world of his day, even though the kingdom he inherited was "a small people" in comparison with the size it once had boasted. Verse 24 gives one more general observation. Antiochus would take his army into the "fattest places" of his own territory and seize wealth from there (which was something his fathers had not done) and then "scatter" this wealth, apparently among the poorer sections of his realm. The probable reason was to gain favor for himself from the majority (the poor) of his subjects. The last part of the verse indicates that he would do this even against the "strong holds" (strongest parts of his domain).

2. His Egyptian campaigns (Dan. 11:25-30a)

Now more detailed information is given about Antiochus' efforts against Egypt to the south. Egypt's king at this time was Ptolemy Philometor (181-145 B.C.), one of two sons of the same Cleopatra who had been married (as part of an unsuccessful scheme) to Ptolemy Epiphanes by Antiochus the Great years before. (This Cleopatra was the sister of Antiochus Epiphanes, making Ptolemy Philometor his nephew.) Both sides now prepared for a major war, and it was joined at Pelusium, located just east of the Nile delta. Thus Antiochus had been able to march the full length of Palestine and even to the border of Egypt without being stopped by the Egyptians. The battle resulted in a clear victory for the Syrians, and a significant reason was that "devices" were worked against the young Ptolemy by his own people (v. 25), those that ate "of the portion of his meat" (v. 26). The last part of verse 26 indicates that though his army would "overflow" (be overpowering) in size (as indeed it was), still it would "fall down slain" in defeat before Antiochus Epiphanes (because of this treachery).

Verse 27 now speaks of these two kings plotting together after the battle, but all the while speaking "lies at one table." History reveals that Antiochus professed friendship for his young nephew after his victory over him, strange as this may seem. The reason was that the Egyptian people at Alexandria, on hearing of Ptolemy's defeat, had put his brother on the Egyptian throne as Ptolemy Euergetes; Antiochus wanted the help of the defeated brother to fight against this new ruler. That the two would speak lies to each other means that Antiochus would make promises to the young man to solicit his help, while not intending to keep them, and the young man in turn would profess to accept them, while all the while not believing his uncle. The figure of speaking lies at the same table is significant because, to the Oriental, deception practiced at a table of hospitality is the lowest in kind. As the close of verse 27 indicates, the plans thus made did not succeed. Antiochus was defeated when he later attempted to march on Alexandria and, as a result, had to return in disappointment to Syria, though he was able to take with him "great riches," as indicated in verse 28.

Verse 28 also indicates that on the way home his heart would be set "against the holy covenant." This is especially significant to note for it is the first indication in the passage concerning Antiochus' treatment of the Jews. History reveals that as Antiochus returned to Syria, he took time in Palestine to work great havoc against the Temple, the religious personnel there, and the ceremonial system — the first of his activities as a figure of the Antichrist. Shortly before his return, there had been a violent reaction by the Jews against the traitorous Menelaus, who had killed the pious Onias, and Antiochus stopped to put down the minor revolt. It is generally accepted that an additional motivation for his deeds was that the Jews provided a convenient way for him to vent his anger for the disappointment he had just experienced in Egypt. He committed savage atrocities and seized many of the valuable objects of the Temple; they are listed in 1 Maccabees 1:21-23 as: "the golden altar, and the candlestick of light, and all the vessels thereof, and the table of the shewbread, and the pouring vessels, and the vials, and the censers of gold, and the vail, and the crowns, and the golden ornaments that were on the front

of the temple." This was only the first of the desecrations that Jerusalem experienced at this man's hand.

Verses 29 and 30a tell of a second campaign against Egypt. It
occurred in 168 B.C. A coalition government had been formed in
Egypt by the two brothers and a sister, and Antiochus determined
to break it. The prediction of the verse is that this time would be
different from the first, and it was; no battle of any kind resulted.
The reason was due to the "ships of Chittim," used by the Romans,
which had come to the aid of the Egyptians. On approaching Alexandria for the intended battle, Antiochus was handed a letter from
the Roman Senate forbidding him to make the attack. The decision
was hard, but Antiochus did not want war with the Romans and
accordingly withdrew. He was fully dejected and even more disap-
pointed than after his first campaign, for he had made great preparation and now was unable to make use of it.

3. Further plunder of the Jews (Dan. 11:30b-35)

Antiochus' forced withdrawal led to a second time of persecution
aganist the Jews in Palestine. Once more he stopped in the land on
his way home to Syria to bring "indignation against the holy covenant" (v. 30). At the time, he had "intelligence with them that
forsake the holy covenant"; that is he schemed with apostate Jews,
urging them fully to forsake their God-given faith and replace it with
the Greek religion. He used "arms" (his army) to work his devastations, as he further polluted the "sanctuary" (Temple), did away
with "the daily sacrifice," and set up the "abomination that makes
desolate." This last expression is basically the same as used in Daniel
9:27 (q.v.) and refers to that which Antiochus erected in the Temple, namely, a substitute altar and/or a statue of Jupiter (Zeus)
Olympius. It represented the substitute form of worship that he
wanted the Jewish people to observe, for he had now outlawed the
Mosaic ordinances. As verse 32 indicates, in effecting all this he
used "flatteries" on those sympathetic to him (who had already forsaken the covenant) in seeking to corrupt them more.

Verse 32 also indicates that at the same time that these Jews were
traitorous in character, there would be others who knew God, who
would be "strong" and do "exploits" against Antiochus. Further,
those who understood the true meaning of what was happening would
"instruct" the many others who were confused. Among these, however, there would be many who would give their lives as a result,
falling by "the sword, and by flame, by captivity, and by spoil many

days" (v. 33; cf. Dan. 8:10-14). During this time, a "little help" would arise (v. 34). This is probably a reference to the emergence of the Maccabees. Mattathias Maccabeus, the father of five sons, refused to offer sacrifice to the Grecian god and instead slew the representative of Antiochus. Then he and his sons, with others who came to join, moved into the mountains and began the famed Maccabean revolt. Many of the group died, but the revolt was effective in stemming the efforts of Antiochus.

Among those who sought to join the movement would be some who would use "flatteries" to do so, meaning that they would be insincere. History shows that as the protest movement grew, it became popular to join and some resorted to subterfuge to be accepted. Verse 35 indicates that all this would be used as a refining process by God. As men of "understanding" and others fell before Antiochus' atrocities, the people would be tried and purged and made white before God. The result would be that all would be drawn closer to God in sincerity of faith; this situation would conttinue until the "time of the end," appointed under God's perfect, allknowing wisdom. In other words, God had a purpose in it all, and until that purpose was completed, this time of suffering would continue.

A double reference in time is likely intended by this last element: a reference to the past time of Antiochus Epiphanes and to the future time of the great tribulation. As will be noted next, the following verses of the chapter concern that future time, and this makes the thought of a transition element here altogether possible. The phrase "time of the end" is regularly used for the great tribulation (see Dan. 11:40; 12:4, 9). Actually, this occasion concerning Antiochus could not be called a "time of the end" itself, for nothing really ended then. It did not finish any "time" or age, but the great tribulation will end the time of the Gentiles, just before Christ sets up His millennial rule when Jews will be in the ascendancy.

D. The Antichrist (Dan. 11:36-45)

The subject now changes from Antiochus to the Antichrist himself. Some of the main reasons for determining this are as follows. (1) The description of this king's character is not true of Antiochus but fits descriptions given elsewhere of the Antichrist. (2) Numerous historical matters are set forth which Antiochus did not do, but there is reason to believe the Antichrist will do them. (3) In verse 40, this one is clearly distinguished from one called "the king of the north"; in view of the use of this term earlier in the chapter, this distinction would be unusual if the person were Antiochus. (4) In this person's time there would be a period of trouble worse than any other in history (Dan. 12:1); this must mean the great tribulation period, when the Antichrist will rule (cf. Matt. 24:21).[5]

1. *The arrogance of the Antichrist (Dan. 11:36-39)*

The first section of this portion gives general information regarding this person; it centers on his extreme arrogance. He will "do according to his will" and thus "magnify himself above every god" and speak "marvellous [astonishing, unbelievable] things against the God of gods." In this he will "prosper till the indignation [Great Tribulation] be accomplished," all of this having been determined ahead of time by God. The element "magnify himself above every god" defines a characteristic that was not true of Antiochus, for he worshiped the gods of Greece. It will be true, however, of the Antichrist, as will all the other elements mentioned.

Verse 37 indicates that this one will not "regard the God of his fathers." This phrase has been understood by some expositors to mean that the Antichrist will be a Jew, arguing on the basis that the phrase "God of his fathers" is often used in the Old Testament in reference to God in His relation to Jews. Since the Antichrist will live in the post-Christian period, however, the phrase could also refer to the God historically worshiped in Rome, which would be the true God as worshiped by the Roman Catholic church. He also will not regard "the desire of women," which may refer to the area of "desire" commonly associated with women, such as mercy, gentleness, kindness. Further, he will not "regard any god" at all; this, again, was not true of Antiochus, but it will be true of the Antichrist. Instead, this one will "magnify himself above all" gods. This statement is similar to one in 2 Thessalonians 2:4, which, speaking of the same person, says he will actually take a seat "in the temple of God, showing himself that he is God."

Verse 38 says that in place of God he will "honour the god of forces [fortresses],"[6] meaning warfare and ability to wage it. Military activity will evidently be high on his priority list, and he will worship this "god" with "gold, and silver, and with precious stones, and

[5]For additional argumentation, see L. J. Wood, *A Commentary on Daniel*, pp. 304, 305.

[6]The term for "forces" is used six other times in this chapter and in all six instances it means "fortress."

pleasant things." The thought is probably that he will need to use valuables of these kinds to finance his costly wars. In this warfare, he will not hesitate to attack the most impregnable "strong holds," and when he has conquered them he will honor the leaders seized by permitting them to "rule over many" (under his own supervision, of course), dividing land among them, no doubt as a way of gaining their allegiance (v. 39). All these matters pertain to the kind of person this one will be. At this point, the subject moves on to activities he undertakes.

2. *The battles of the Antichrist (Dan. 11:40-45)*

a. Initial battle (Dan. 11:40). Now follows one of the most significant passages of the Bible concerning the battles of the Antichrist. In verse 40 a battle is described as occurring between him and two united opponents, who are designated by terms from the earlier portion of the chapter — "king of the north" and "king of the south." Because these are the same names as used in verses 5-20, it is logical to relate them. Since, however, the time involved is that of the Antichrist, the political situation then existent could well make a change in the specific references. In terms of today, the "king of the south" could still be the leader of Egypt, since Egypt significantly serves as the leading nation of the Arab bloc. "King of the north," however, could hardly refer to the Syrian ruler, for Syria is not sufficiently important in world affairs to qualify. This term, therefore, is commonly thought to refer to the leader of Russia;[7] this fits the world situation today, for Russia forms an important bloc with Arabs against the Jews.

Furthermore, the idea of a battle between the Antichrist and this Russian-Arab bloc fits the thought already seen under Daniel 9:27. There it was observed that at the beginning of the tribulation period, the Antichrist will make a treaty with Israel. It is logical to think that the Russian-Arab bloc would sooner or later make a move in retaliation, such as is indicated in this verse. They would see the Antichrist as a latecomer to an old grudge with Israel, and he would have to be defeated before the grudge could be further pursued. The Antichrist, in his interest for world power, would be prepared to counter such an attack.

In view of the fact that the Antichrist will break his covenant with Israel at the midpoint of the seven-year period (see Dan. 9:27), one

---

[7]For discussion, see L. J. Wood, *A Commentary on Daniel,* pp. 308-310.

can even conjecture the time of this battle. It would fit well at the time just before the covenant is broken. This conclusion follows from the fact that the Antichrist would want to maintain the covenant as long as the Russian-Arab opposition continued; but should that come to an end, then the need for the covenant would also end, and he could be expected to break it.

The nature of the battle is set forth clearly and succinctly. The two uniting forces would come against the Antichrist, using chariots, horsemen, and ships (all probably representative of modern weapons, which were completely unknown by either writer or reader in Daniel's day). "He" (meaning the Antichrist, for either of the opposing leaders would be identified by his appropriate title) would be able to "overflow" and "pass over" like a flooding river of water. So then the Antichrist will win the battle and will have no further need of the treaty with Israel.

b. Seizure of Palestine (Dan. 11:41-45). Having defeated this major bloc, the Antichrist will be at liberty to take Palestine for himself (v. 41). He will enter "into the glorious land," meaning Palestine (cf. v. 16 and Dan. 8:9), and there he will overthrow many. It should be observed that the word "countries," inserted here in the King James Version, is not in the Hebrew. "Many" refers to the Jewish people, large numbers of whom the Antichrist will kill when he invades their land. They will find that this former friend has become their greatest enemy, and they will be slaughtered as they try to keep him from conquering their land. It will be at this time, no doubt, that he will order the "sacrifice and the oblation to cease" (Dan. 9:27), since he will be able to enter Jerusalem itself and enforce his will as he pleases. This means that Israel's splendid air force and army, as strong as it is today, will be crushed by the power and expertise of this man and his army as the land falls before him.

The second half of verse 41 indicates that he will not continue his efforts to conquer toward the southeast; thus he will not move on into the areas of Edom, Moab, and Ammon. Instead (v. 42) he will march southeastward, down into Egypt, whose army he will have already defeated in the major battle just noted. Egypt will fall easily and also Libya (to the west) and then Ethiopia, or perhaps better, Nubia (to the south); so he will gain control of all northeastern Africa.

Verse 44 says that he will now hear bad news "out of the east and out of the north." This will prompt him to "go forth with great fury to destroy, and utterly to make away many." Some expositors believe this news will concern an army of some 200 million, mainly Chinese, who will have come for a portion of the spoils of the Middle East, having heard of the Antichrist's victory over the Russian-Arab bloc. This explanation is based especially on Revelation 9:16 and 16:12. Others, however, believe these will be tidings out of Palestine itself, possibly that troops left there by the Antichrist have suffered serious reverses at the hands of Jews who refused to consider themselves defeated yet. Which view is best is not easily determined, but it may be observed that Revelation 9:16 and 16:12 could refer to an army of demons, rather than men. The figure of 200 million for a human army is almost incredible. Whatever the correct view, the Antichrist will hear disturbing news and return to Palestine to bring remedy. He will then be able to annihilate completely the enemy that has caused the rumors. This argues farther against the view that this enemy is an army of 200 million. One cannot help but wonder if the Antichrist, for all his power, could possibly be so successful against an army this large. However, he could easily put down an uprising of the Jews.

Verse 45 now brings this account of warfare to a close. The Antichrist is said now to be able to "plant the tabernacles [tents] of his palace between the seas in the glorious holy mountain." The "seas" would be the Dead Sea and the Mediterranean Sea, and the mountain would be Mount Zion, or Jerusalem. For an ancient conqueror to place his tents in a conquered territory signified his complete conquest of it. He could direct his activities from them, and they also served as symbols of the conquest he had made. Thus, the Antichrist here is said to have made a complete conquest of Palestine for himself. In light of Zechariah 13:8, 9, which says two-thirds of all Jews of the day will be killed at this time, it may be concluded that this number will now have been destroyed by the Antichrist. This time of devastation, then, will indeed be a day of "Jacob's trouble." The same passage in Zechariah states that the purpose of God in this is to refine His people so that they will truly acknowledge Him as their God.

The last phrase of verse 45 indicates the end that will finally come on the Antichrist. "He shall come to his end, and none shall help him." This will take place after the war with the Jews has been completed, when Christ comes in power to deliver His people at last. This coming in power is pictured especially in Revelation 19:11-21. At that time the entire army of the Antichrist will be killed instantaneously by Christ, though not before both the Antichrist and his helper, the false prophet, are cast alive into the lake of fire (Rev. 19:20). This makes the end of the Antichrist and the Roman empire abrupt indeed. (Cf. discussion under Dan. 7:9-11, 26.)

For Further Study

1. Read articles in a Bible dictionary or encyclopedia on: (a) Ptolemy, (b) Seleucus or Seleucids.
2. To whom do the terms "king of the south" and "king of the north" in Daniel 11:5-20 refer?
3. In two columns, make a list of the Ptolemaic and Seleucid kings from Daniel 11:5-20, keeping them contemporaneous. Draw a line between those which are related to each other in some manner in these verses.
4. What is the main significance of describing Antiochus Epiphanes at such length in Daniel 11:21-35? Describe him as a person.
5. Briefly describe his two campaigns against Egypt.
6. What did he do in Palestine after each of these campaigns?
7. List the main features set forth regarding the Antichrist in Daniel 11:36-39.
8. Describe the conflict set forth in Daniel 11:40, and relate it in time to the seventieth week of Daniel 9:27.
9. Where will the Antichrist make military conquest after this battle?
10. What do Daniel 11:44, 45 indicate as to the extent of his conquest over the Jews in Israel?

Chapter 12

The Fourth Vision: The Great Tribulation

There is no change in basic subject matter from chapter 11 to chapter 12. In fact, the heavenly visitor's message to Daniel continues without break through verse 4 of this chapter, making his uninterrupted message extend totally from 10:20 through 12:4. In verses 6 and 8, questions were asked by another heavenly messenger and by Daniel; these in turn prompted the first messenger to speak further in verses 7 and 9 to 12.

A. Some General Matters (Dan. 12:1-3)

Daniel's visitor continued to speak of the period when the Antichrist would rule, but he did so now more from the point of view of the people ruled rather than from that of the ruler. The period is properly called the great tribulation. This follows especially from three factors: first, the thought continues without break from the close of chapter 11, where the subject was the Antichrist, who will rule during the great tribulation; second, it is logical to identify this period with the "time of the end" of Daniel 11:40, where the reference is to the great tribulation; third, Jesus refers to this passage in Matthew 24:21, where the context identifies the period as the great tribulation.

It should be realized, then, that the "time" referred to in verse 1 will not follow the demise of the Antichrist, mentioned in Daniel 11:45, but will be the same period as that during which he brings his oppressions.

1. *Michael's protection of Israel (Dan. 12:1)*

The thought of verse 1 is that during this tribulation time, Michael will "stand up" to aid Israel, in keeping with his general assignment as noted under Daniel 10:13, 20. In fact, this general assignment is indicated here by the words "which standeth [as guard] for the

LAST-DAY EVENTS

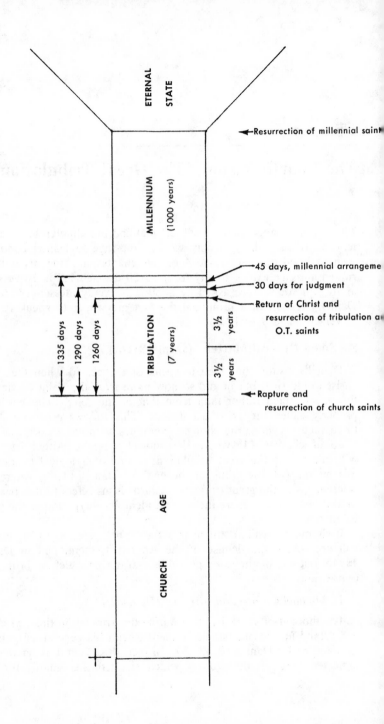

children of thy people." The reason Michael must do this is because of the climactic "time of trouble" which then will come on the whole world. Because of his help, Daniel's "people" will be "delivered" namely, those "found written in the book" of life (cf. Exod. 32:32; Ps. 69:28; Luke 10:20; Rev. 20:12). The period of the Antichrist's rule, then, will be a time of suffering unparalleled in human history, but the Jewish people will be delivered from a substantial part of this affliction[1] due to the intervention of their specially assigned angel, Michael.

2. *The posttribulational resurrection (Dan. 12:2, 3)*

Verse 3 speaks of a resurrection, and some expositors see it as a spiritual resurrection, namely the change one experiences when he is saved, thus paralleling the thought just expressed, "Every one that shall be found written in the book." This cannot be correct, however, because some of those resurrected find themselves consigned to "shame and everlasting contempt." The words used, as well as the context, point rather to a literal resurrection from "the dust of the earth." The preceding verse, in speaking of the tribulation period, has left open the question of the status of righteous Jews who have died under the crushing hand of the Antichrist. This verse now answers by saying that they will not be omitted from the great blessings of the millennial rule of Christ that will follow (as indicated especially in the first vision, Dan. 7:13, 14, 27); they will be resurrected at the close of the tribulation time and before that millennial period will begin (cf. Rev. 20:4-6).

Some of these will be resurrected unto "everlasting life," but others "to shame and everlasting contempt." From this verse alone, one might think that the resurrection of both groups will occur at this posttribulational, premillennial time. This cannot be, however, because Revelation 20:4-6, 12-15 shows that the resurrection of the first group will precede the millennium while that of the second will follow it. Daniel 12:2, written at a much earlier time than Revelation 20, is merely giving a general indication regarding the two aspects of the resurrection without pointing out the time distinction between them, leaving that to the later revelation. A paraphrase of the verse would be, "And many that sleep in the dust of the earth shall awake (to have part with the living righteous in millennial benefits); these, truly, shall be to everlasting life, but others (of the sleepers, who do

---

[1]This affliction is very likely represented by the broken seals, blown trumpets, and poured-out bowls of wrath in Revelation (see chaps. 6, 8, 9, 11, 16).

not awake at this time, but only after the millennium) shall be to shame and everlasting contempt."

The thought of verse 3 is that those of this resurrected group (as well as those "found written in the book" and still alive at the close of the tribulation) who have turned "many to righteousness" will be counted "wise." The time in view surely is the tribulation period. In other words, those who have witnessed to other Jews concerning God's truth and helped them place faith in Christ as their Messiah during this time of trouble will be counted "wise" in the sight of God, and they will be made to "shine as the brightness" of the stars in the firmament forever. Though the special time in view is the tribulation week, the application is good for any day, as Jesus illustrated, especially in Matthew 13:43.

B. Tribulation Chronology (Dan. 12:4-12)

The visitor's uninterrupted message ends with verse 4. He spoke further in following verses, but mainly in response to specific questions that were asked him. The general theme concerns the chronology of last-day events.

1. *A first indication (Dan. 12:4)*

The first indication regarding the chronology of the great tribulation is that this period would be far in the future of Daniel's own day. For this reason, Daniel was told to "shut up the words" he had just written "and seal the book" so that it might be carefully preserved for those who would later need its information. The identity of this book must be at least the collection of Daniel's records of all four visions and probably the entire book of Daniel. At what point in his closing years Daniel wrote his book is not revealed, but he probably was already bringing it to a close by this time, since he was now about eighty-four years of age. The phrase, "time of the end," is the same as used in Daniel 11:35, 40, where it was seen to refer especially to the great tribulation; the same surely is true here. It will be at that time that the information Daniel wrote will be particularly pertinent. People will be running "to and fro" looking for such information, and they will be able to find it in this preserved record from Daniel, so that "knowledge shall be increased."

2. *A second indication (Dan. 12:5-10)*

a. Indication proper (Dan. 12:5-7). A second indication concerning tribulational chronology is given only after an intervening question asked of Daniel's visitor (vv. 4, 5). It was voiced by another heavenly messenger (one of two seen by Daniel as they stood on opposite sides of the Tigris River) and addressed to "the man clothed in linen" (who must be the same visitor). This one was now seen "upon [or, above] the waters of the river." Earlier this visitor had been active on the bank of the river, ministering to Daniel, as was noted (Dan. 10:10, 16, 18), but apparently he moved to this position out over the river. His ability to remain in this gravity-defying position is perhaps intended to symbolize his supernatural power and authority. The question asked him was, "How long shall it be to the end of these wonders?" In other words, how long would this time last when the wonders that had been described would transpire?

As the visitor prepared to give an answer, he raised both "his right hand and his left hand unto heaven." This was a gesture to show solemnity and importance for an oath (cf. Gen. 14:22; Deut. 32:40). Normally only one hand would be raised; two hands in this instance indicated special stress. Further emphasis is lent by the indication that the messenger "swore by him that lives for ever," meaning God.

The answer given after this indication of emphasis has two parts. The first is a repetition of the formula for time used in Daniel 7:25: "time, times, and an half." As noted under 7:25, this means three-and-a-half years, the exact equivalent of the last half of the tribulation week, following the breaking of the covenant by the Antichrist (Dan. 9:27). This duration agrees, then, with the period already seen, when the Antichrist brings his vicious attack against the Jews in Palestine.

The other part of the answer is given in the words, "When he shall have accomplished to scatter the power of the holy people." The thought is that this time of trouble would continue as long as it would take to break the power (self-will) of the Jews. This part of the answer, then, gives the reason for God's permitting these atrocities of the Antichrist against the Jews: namely, to break their spirit of self-sufficiency. Parallel passages (e.g., Zech. 12:7-10; 13:8, 9) indicate that this will be necessary so that the Jews will be humbled before God and made willing to accept Christ as their rightful Messiah-king. The two parts of the total answer, then, combine to say that it will take the Antichrist exactly three-and-a-half years to bring the Jews to the state of humiliation where this willingness will be evidenced.

b. *Parenthetical thoughts (Dan. 12:8-10).* Verses 8 to 10 stand somewhat parenthetically in the general chronological thought being developed. In verse 8, Daniel expressed wonderment on his part as he asked, "What shall be the end of these things?" The word he used for "end" is different from that employed by the heavenly messenger in verse 6 and means, "latter end." Daniel's question, then, referred primarily to the closing events of this tribulation time. He was puzzled about how this terrible time of suffering would close. Then verse 9 tells how the grand messenger mildly rebuked Daniel for his curiosity, telling him that he should be satisfied with what he had already been told. He should go his way, being content to know that the words revealed to him were securely preserved ("closed up and sealed") and therefore would be available for people to know in this future time of trouble. It is clear, then, that Daniel wanted to know more information than God saw necessary; in this he was like many Christians today: they also want to know more about last things than God has revealed. They, like Daniel, should rest content with what has been set forth.

The grand messenger added a bit of information as to an important accomplishment during the tribulation time. He said, "Many shall be purified, and made white, and tried [refined]," no doubt by the suffering experienced (v. 10). Significantly, the words here used are identical with those regarding people during the days of suffering under Antiochus Epiphanes (Dan. 11:35). The thought is that as that earlier time served to refine people in respect to their relation to God, so this later time will accomplish the same. The remainder of the verse indicates that while this refinement will be the experience of righteous Jews, the unrighteous ones will continue in their wickedness. But, added the messenger, these unrighteous ones will not understand the significance of what was then happening to the Jews, whereas the "wise" (refined ones) will know.

3. *A third indication (Dan. 12:11, 12)*

The grand messenger then gave a third chronological indication about the tribulation; it has two parts. He said, first, that from the time that "the daily sacrifice shall be taken away, and the abomination that makes desolate set up" (in other words the middle of the tribulation week, Dan. 9:27) will be 1,290 days. The termination point of these days is not indicated. One might assume it to be the end of the last half of the week, but a period of 1,290 days is too long by 30 days; also, this half of the week has already been indicated to be three-and-a-half years (which is 1,260 days, figuring 30-day months, as sustained by a comparison of vv. 6 and 14 in Rev. 12 and vv. 2 and 3 in Rev. 11). The question must be asked, then, as to the significance of the 30 additional days.

A clue comes from Matthew 25:31-46, which describes a time of judgment by Christ immediately after He comes in power at the close of this period. The purpose of this judgment is to determine who will be permitted to enter and enjoy the millennial period. But such an act of judgment will take a little time, and the added 30 days here in view would seem appropriate for that period. This would mean that the full time in view of these 1,290 days would be from the middle of the tribulation week until the completion of this time of judgment.

The second part of the indication comes in verse 12. The messenger next spoke of 1,335 days and said that those who wait until the completion of this time will be "blessed." This figure is 45 days longer than the preceding one and 75 days more than the duration of the last half of the tribulation week. What is the significance of this additional period of time? The word, "blessed" may give a clue. There will be blessing for those who come to the conclusion of this period. This suggests the thought that the millennium will actually start on that day. Those who have passed the judgment of Christ during the preceding 30 days, will be those who attain to the millennium, after 45 more days. What will be the purpose of these additional days? It may be the time necessary for setting up the governmental organization for the millennial rule. The true and full border of Israel (from the River of Egypt to the Euphrates, Gen. 15:18) will have to be established, and there will be need for appointments of personnel as well. Christ will be supreme King, but He will no doubt employ subordinates to serve under Him. A period of 45 days would seem reasonable as a length of time in which to accomplish such matters.

C. Closing Advice to Daniel (Dan. 12:13)

Daniel closed his book by including a word of advice from the grand messenger to himself. He said that he was bidden to go his way "till the end be" (meaning, "cease being anxious over these matters for as long as you live"). Daniel was to rest satisfied with knowing as much as had been told him, rather than fretting and wishing that all his questions had been answered. This is good advice for all God's people.

Then the messenger instructed Daniel that he would "rest" (in death) and finally stand in his "lot at the end of the days." The word for "lot" here is used in the sense of "inheritance lot" (cf. Judg. 1:3; Col. 1:12). Daniel would receive his portion of inheritance "at the end of the days," meaning at the end of the days dealt with in the context, the tribulation days. The relation to verse 12 is that, thus having received his lot at the close of the tribulation days, Daniel would have it in time to enjoy the blessings of the millennial days. An important truth is implied in this statement. If Daniel is to be resurrected at this time, then other Old Testament saints will likely be resurrected at the same time, thus giving evidence regarding the probable time for the resurrection of Old Testament saints.

And so with the fact settled that he had learned all he was going to and that he would truly have his part in the blessedness of this future occasion, Daniel ceased to write. He probably was taken in death to be with his Lord soon after this time.

For Further Study

1. What will Michael do in behalf of Israel during the great tribulation?
2. What two times of resurrection are referred to in Daniel 12:2? Who will rise from the dead each of these times?
3. What seem to be the significances of the three different time periods indicated in this chapter: 1,260 days, 1,290 days, and 1,335 days?
4. What evidence may be drawn from Daniel 12:13 that Old Testament saints will rise from the dead following the great tribulation?